Having People, Having Heart

Having People, Having Heart

Charity, Sustainable Development, and Problems of Dependence in Central Uganda

CHINA SCHERZ

The University of Chicago Press
Chicago and London

China Scherz is assistant professor of anthropology at Reed College.

The University of Chicago Press, Chicago 60637
The University of Chicago Press, Ltd., London
© 2014 by The University of Chicago
All rights reserved. Published 2014.
Printed in the United States of America

23 22 21 20 19 18 17 16 15 14   1 2 3 4 5

ISBN-13: 978-0-226-11953-3 (cloth)
ISBN-13: 978-0-226-11967-0 (paper)
ISBN-13: 978-0-226-11970-0 (e-book)
DOI: 10.7208/chicago/9780226119700.001.0001

Library of Congress Cataloging-in-Publication Data
Scherz, China, author.
  Having people, having heart: charity, sustainable development, and
problems of dependence in Central Uganda / China Scherz.
    pages; cm
  Includes bibliographical references and index.
  ISBN 978-0-226-11953-3 (cloth: alk. paper) — ISBN 978-0-226-11967-0
(pbk.: alk. paper) — ISBN 978-0-226-11970-0 (e-book) 1. Charities—
Uganda. 2. Non-governmental organizations—Uganda. 3. Hope Child
(Organization: Uganda) 4. Mercy House (Uganda) 5. Sustainable
development—Uganda. 6. Charity—Moral and ethical aspects. I. Title.
  HV447.S34 2014
  338.96761—dc23   2013035830

♾ This paper meets the requirements of ANSI/NISO Z39.48-1992
(Permanence of Paper).

CONTENTS

ACKNOWLEDGMENTS

Among the first things one learns to say in Luganda is *webale*, thank you, and one finds oneself using this word nearly constantly in greeting, in expressing gratitude, in expressing gratitude for the gratitude that others have shown to you. It may never be possible to reciprocate the many gifts of assistance, hospitality, and wisdom that have been shown and given to me since I began working on this book seven years ago. I hope that these gifts were given from generous hearts expecting only my gratitude in return, or that my mentors and friends will continue to be patient with my long delay in reciprocity.

My greatest debts are clearly to those in Uganda who have helped me with my work and who have taught me how to depend on others. I thank all the members of the family I first stayed with in Uganda, particularly Evarist, Martha, Rose, Philip, Elizabeth, Jacqueline, Prossy, and Flavia, for opening their home to me and for being my first teachers in Uganda. I also thank Diana and her daughter Vicki, who both lived with us in Sebanda. Thanks also to Winifred Babiyre and all the teachers at the Kampala City Language center, especially Ven Kitone, who not only taught me Luganda but also, through her dear friendship and example, taught me what it means to have a giving heart.

I owe a deep debt of gratitude to the staff members, volunteers, donors, and participants of the NGO I call Hope Child, who allowed me to join them in their work. I especially want to thank the two Hope Child Sebanda field office staff members, whom I call Martin Mugerwa and Sarah Nassali, for their unfailing patience with my presence. I also thank the many people of Sebanda who welcomed me and my husband, Paul, into their communities during my research. *Mwebale nnyo okunyamba. Sikisoboka okukola kunyonereza kino si mmwe. Nsubira nti kijja kubayamba edda.* (Thank you all for helping me. I could not have completed this research without you. I hope that someday it may be of use to you.) I also thank the members of the religious order I call the Franciscan Sisters of Africa, who welcomed me into their lives and work. I especially thank those I call Sisters Jane, Valentine, Caroline, and Sylvia for all they taught me about what it means to dedicate one's life. I also thank the two Peace Corps volunteers I call Ruth Petersen and Monica Richards and all the residents of Mercy House who welcomed Paul and me on so many occasions. I also thank Josephine Namirimu, who worked as my research assistant during my return visit to Mercy House in 2010. I also owe special acknowledgment to the staff members of the foundations in the Netherlands for generously sharing their time with me and for their ongoing support of Hope Child and Mercy House.

I do not have words to express my gratitude to George Mpanga, who has worked with me over the past six years as a research assistant and translator. This project would have been impossible without the many months we spent traveling together on foot or by motorcycle taxi along the muddy lanes of the Sebanda subcounty, talking with people and mulling over the ideas that appear in this book; without the countless hours he spent transcribing interviews in longhand in a borrowed office in a trading center; and without our ongoing correspondence. I also thank Lawrence Waswa and Zubeda Katono for their work on the Sebanda village survey.

The thoughts that emerged out of all these conversations in Uganda and Europe were deeply shaped by further discussions with those closer to home. At the Universities of California at Berkeley and San Francisco I benefited from the unfailing guidance of a group of extraordinary teachers, mentors, and colleagues. Vincanne Adams, Lawrence Cohen, Jennifer Johnson-Hanks, Dorothy Porter, and Paul Rabinow supported me throughout the research, and each also made distinct contributions to this project in particular and to my development as a scholar more generally. I especially express my gratitude to Vincanne Adams for the extraordinary care she put into helping me develop and refine the arguments and writing. I also thank Natal Ayiga, Aubrey Bauer, Gay Becker, Erica Bornstein, Betsey Brada, Robert Brightman, Douglas Buser, David Claremont, Jennifer Cole, Jean Comaroff, Jonathan Earle, James Ferguson, Courtney Handman, Shana Harris, Judith Justice, Tabitha Kanogo, Sharon Kaufman, Mike Keen, Stephan Kloos, Paul Kollman, Cecelia Lynch, Charlene Makley, Liisa Malkki, Suepattra May, Gail McGuire, Edward Miguel, Katherine Miller, James Ntozi, Abena Dove Osseo-Asare, Michal Ran-Rubin, Charles Rwabukwali, Joel Robbins, Paul Silverstein, Scott Stonington, Lila M. Stromer, LaShandra Sullivan, Ann Swidler, Anwen Tormey, Rebecca Torstrick, Todd Whitmore,

Suzanne Wint, the Chicago African Studies Workshop, the Notre Dame Africa Studies Working Group, and the Berkeley Center for African Studies. I also express my sincere appreciation to David Brent, Priya Nelson, Alice Bennett, and all of the production staff at the University of Chicago Press for making the publication of this book so smooth.

A National Science Foundation Graduate Research Fellowship, a Foreign Language Area Studies Summer Language Fellowship, a Berkeley Center for African Studies Rocca Scholarship, a University of California at San Francisco (UCSF) Kozloff Fellowship, a UCSF President's Dissertation Year Fellowship, and the UCSF Graduate Division and Graduate Students Association provided the financial support for the research and writing of this book. Portions of chapter 6 have appeared in *American Ethnologist* (2013).

Finally, I thank my family and friends for all they have done to support me. I thank my father, Charlie Star, for encouraging me to take risks; my sister, Summer Star, for her daily encouragement and conversation; and Brian Cassidy, Jani Davis, Karen Fong, Jeanne Sachs, Edith Sachs, Aletha Schelby, Carl and Betsy Scherz, and Billy Steele for all they have done to keep me going. Most important, I thank my husband, Paul Scherz, who has supported me in unimaginable ways and who has lived and thought through this project with me from beginning to end. Finally I thank our children, Iggy and Lucy, for bringing so much joy into our lives.

I am unable to express my thanks to the person who shaped me and my work most deeply, since this work was written in memory of my mother, Denise Evans, whose strength, grace, and faith therein continue to astonish me.

ONE

Introduction: What We Are Doing Here Is Not Charity

"What we are doing here is not charity," Sarah Nassali[1] explained to me as she described the suite of community-based orphan support programs she was managing at Hope Child. The frequency with which she and other employees of Ugandan nongovernmental organizations (NGOs) distinguished their work as being something other than charity, and the lengths they went to avoid creating dependence on foreign funding, evinced an international push for more sustainable, community-owned development (Rahnema 1992; Stirrat and Henkel 1997; Green 2000; Cooke and Kothari 2001; Paley 2001; Li 2007; Kremer and Miguel 2007; Swidler and Watkins 2009). Sustainable development projects, like those run by Hope Child, are intended to have an impact beyond the lives of the projects themselves, and they rely on creating strong community institutions that will exist after the NGO and its resources leave. Nassali's comments not only indexed this new way of thinking about development, but also spoke to the marginal position of the charitable gift—the "handout"—and the specter of dependence within the contemporary philanthropic field.

Hope Child's attempts to avoid handouts ultimately caused tension between its field office staff and the program's beneficiaries and volunteers. Whereas Hope Child staff members were interested in creating support groups for grandparents caring for orphans and in building community-run Early Childhood Development centers for children under age eight, local people wanted farm implements, livestock, school fees, and mattresses. Despite Hope Child's claim that these beneficiaries were the "owners" of the project, they were not able to persuade Hope Child to spend more than 6 percent of its US$375,000 program budget on tangible inputs. While the Hope Child staff, and the donor foundations that supported them, saw refusing handouts as part of a strategy to avoid aid dependence and to promote programs that would yield lasting benefits, the beneficiaries saw these choices as suspect refusals to redistribute wealth, and they echoed a refrain familiar across the African continent: the NGO staff was likely "eating the money" (Bayart 1989).

This book focuses on these tensions and accusations and asks what gifts and dependence, and attempts to avoid them, mean in a community where patron-client relationships serve as a primary ethical compass. In the chapters that follow, I articulate a central international debate on the most effective means for bringing about economic development and social justice, a debate that pits charity against sustainability. In my analysis of this debate I highlight the judgments that rural Baganda[2] make about the programs that result from these alternate ethical orientations.

Interdependence, Development, and Ethics in Central Uganda

Interdependence

One of the core premises of this book is that ideals of independence and self-reliance, which lie at the heart of sustainable development, are socially and historically constructed and, more specifically, that this well-established claim has important implications for rethinking the contemporary ethics of international development and philanthropy. In opposition to the tremendous value placed on independence and self-reliance in many Western cultures, in much of the world personhood is achieved through relationships with other people (Shweder and Bourne 1982; Markus and Kitayama 1991). This is not to imply that Kiganda actors do not act as authors of their own futures; rather, their strategies of self-making involve creating and using networks (which are often hierarchical) to secure support (which is often material).[3]

In Buganda, ethics of hierarchical interdependence occupy an important place in local moral economies, particularly among the rural poor. These ethics of interdependence, which I discuss in greater detail in chapter 2, mean that people with resources stand to gain from their relationships with those who have less; that they have a moral obligation to take on clients; and that people with limited resources must actively try to attach themselves to others as dependents. Within this system, one increases one's standing and sense of being a full person by attaching oneself to others and by acquiring clients, not by becoming "independent." To be dependent on another is not a sign of destitution; as Patrick Chabal and Jean-

Pascal Daloz write, "The truly destitute are those without patrons" (Chabal and Daloz 1999, 42).

The multiplicity of patrons actively competing for clients, and the clients' freedom to move from one patron to another should the first fail to meet their needs, builds a critical flexibility into these relations. Thus, as James Ferguson notes, "The freedom that existed in such a social world (and it was not inconsiderable) came not from independence, but from a plurality of opportunities for dependence" (Ferguson 2013, 226). By acquiring a wide range of patrons, clients are assured of "having people" who can assist them in a variety of ways (Smith 2004), and they also gain a measure of insurance against the fickle fortunes, and hearts, of their patrons.

Ferguson has recently written about the conflict between Western ideals of development and the demands made by Africans seeking to enter into hierarchical relations of patronage. He notes that given Amartya Sen's definition of development as an increase in human freedom "to declare for dependence, to wish for it, to seek it, seems to be a wish for one's own devaluation, and even dehumanization" (Ferguson 2013, 225). This position is troubling for Ferguson, and for me, given the frequency with which such "declarations of dependence" are made by poor people in Africa who are attempting to improve their lives (Ferguson 2013).

In line with Ferguson's recent work, my research on the interactions between charity, sustainable development, and Kiganda ethics of interdependence seeks to unsettle our assumptions about the moral valence of dependence in contemporary sub-Saharan Africa. In so doing, I join Ferguson and other scholars, including sociologists Ann Swidler and Susan Watkins (2007), in their efforts to shift the discussion of "wealth-in-people" in Africa from its focus on why patrons sought to amass dependents (Kopytoff and Miers 1977; Miller 1988; Vansina 1990; Guyer and Belinga 1995) toward why dependents seek to attach themselves to patrons—and the increasing difficulty of securing such patronage in the contemporary moment.

The Gift

In taking up these issues of charity and dependence, one is confronted by the theoretical position—taken by authors such as Mary Douglas, Marcel Mauss, and Pierre Bourdieu—that while charity benefits the giver, it necessarily harms the standing of the person who receives it. Understanding this claim requires some sense of Marcel Mauss's writings on gift exchange. In The Gift, first published as an essay in 1925, Mauss famously posited three obligations—to give, to receive, and to reciprocate—and argued that it is through these cycles of exchange that social relationships are established and maintained and that social status is secured and defended. While Mauss's original intent was to explain the history of the separation between self-interest and altruism, *The Gift* is often read as advancing an agonistic theory of exchange in which social actors are primarily interested in securing power and prestige through their generosity, which humiliates recipients who find themselves unable to make a return gift, thus making the potlatch a model for all exchange. Jonathan Parry (1986) argues that this common misreading of Mauss is shaped by Malinowski's theories of exchange, which are based on a balanced, self-interested dyad and depend on a vision of humans as rational actors, constantly seeking to maximize their transactions.[4]

It is with this Malinowskian reading in mind that Mary Douglas and Pierre Bourdieu described the inherent violence of charity. In her essay "No Free Gifts," the foreword to a 1990 edition of Mauss's *The Gift*, Douglas writes, "Though we laud charity as a Christian virtue we know that it wounds" (Douglas 1990, vii). Given the impossibility of reciprocity, Douglas argues that charity yields only the pain of unrepayable gift debt and "does nothing to enhance solidarity" (vii). To some degree, Douglas's analysis reflects Mauss's own writings on charity. In a section titled "Moral Conclusions," he writes, "Charity is still wounding for him who has accepted it, and the whole tendency of our morality is to strive to do away with the unconscious and injurious patronage of the rich almsgiver" (Mauss [1925] 1990, 65). While developing a theory of exchange informed by a dynamic and diachronic theory of practice, Bourdieu maintained this rigid understanding of the structural necessity of reciprocity and, along with it, the moral critique of charity. From *Outline of a Theory of Practice* (1977) to *Pascalian Meditations* (2000), unrepayable alms serve as one of Bourdieu's main examples of symbolic violence.[5]

There are certainly situations in Uganda and elsewhere where gifts are made either partially or primarily to secure a return, whether in the form of material reciprocity, as is often the case when the poor give to the rich, or in the more elusive yet no less significant form of gratitude, loyalty, respect, obedience, or conversion, yet this is not always the case. In opposition to structural arguments concerning the *necessary* violence of charity and the ubiquity of "gift debt," this books calls for closer attention to the role that particular sociohistorical conjunctures play in shaping how givers and receivers understand these acts of charitable giving.[6] In line with Maurice Godelier (1999), I argue that while gifts do entail the simultaneous production of inequality and solidarity, these opposing dynamics are brought together in a wide range of situations that influence the effects of any given exchange. In this argument I hope to challenge distinctions between self-interest and altruism, which have shaped many of the contemporary readings of Mauss that focus on the self-interested nature of calculated reciprocal gift exchanges (Blau 1964; Firth 1967; Douglas 1990). These readings ignore Mauss's fundamental insight that the division between self-interest and altruism is a product of modern economics (Parry 1986), not a timeless truth. There is much at stake in this argument, not only for the anthropology of exchange, but also for more pragmatic discussions concerning the effects and moral valence of philanthropic giving.

Development, Humanitarianism, and Charity

This discussion of charity expands a set of anthropological conversations about aid that until recently (Bornstein 2012) largely centered on development and humanitarianism. While humanitarianism, and to a lesser extent development, originally emerged in relation to notions of Christian charity, there are important differences between development, humanitarianism, and charity that extend beyond—but are not necessarily congruent with—a distinction between the religious and the secular. These differences can be seen in their differing orientations toward time, hierarchy, the motivation for providing aid, the figure of the recipient, and assumptions about human agency.

In terms of time, development is shaped by a future-oriented teleological narrative, which envisions humanity moving toward a common future of modernity and mass consumption (Rist 2003). Humanitarianism, by contrast, is oriented toward the immediate present, the emergency, the crisis, and it operates with only limited thought for the future (Calhoun 2010). While the temporality of charity is closer to that of humanitarianism than to that of development in its primary goal for the intrinsic good of an act of giving in the immediate present (Scherz 2013), it does not require an exceptional moment of crisis (Redfield 2010) and may in many cases be oriented toward ordinary, not extraordinary, suffering.

These logics of care also differ on questions of hierarchy. In its most idealized form, development is conceived as eliminating hierarchy. This, of course, requires us to ignore the fact that capitalism relies on inequality as the engine for competition and growth and that it by no means guarantees that everyone will benefit equally from the system (Rist 2003). Humanitarianism also seeks to eliminate hierarchy, but here this operation is per-

categorizing all people as sharing a common humanity while
participating in the politics of life, which ironically creates
es hierarchies between the providers and recipients of aid and
..ı expatriate volunteers and their local counterparts (Fassin 2007;
Redfield 2012). By contrast, charity sees poverty and inequality as persis-
tent qualities of a fallen world, unlikely to be completely resolved through
human action.

This speaks to key variations in the sense of human agency and the envisioned scope or reach of aid. Development practitioners seek to remake
the world and its subjects through planned interventions, be they dams or
new markets. Although shifts away from development and toward "poverty
reduction" have tempered some of the enthusiasm found in the works of
early development theorists like Walt Whitman Rostow (1960), the hope
persists that the world can be made substantially different through human
action. While the scope and aim of humanitarian assistance were originally quite limited, the recent conjoining of humanitarianism with human
rights and military intervention has greatly expanded the scope of these
previously limited operations (Rieff 2002). As I argue in chapters 4 and 6,
givers of charity often conceive of the worldly effects of their gifts and their
own ability to change the future in far more limited terms (Scherz 2013).

Charity also differs from both humanitarianism and development in the
roles that religious injunctions and divine exchange play in motivating the
charitable gift. The people described in this book who made charitable gifts
thought of these gifts as offerings to God made as acts of supplication, as
thanksgiving for blessings received, and, most profoundly, as thanksgiving
for the unrepayable gift of salvation. These motivations not only complicate notions of reciprocity, as I discuss in detail in chapter 4; they also differ
substantially from the motivations that lie behind aid given for the sake of
development or humanitarianism. While ideas of expressing gratitude toward a less specified force may move individual donors to give, both development and humanitarianism are more often influenced by a wide range of
secular motivations that, obviously, vary depending on the actors involved.
These motivations might include such disparate factors as notions of justice
and human rights, the desire to create new markets, or attempts to secure
geopolitical alliances. Thinking about charity as an exchange with God also
helps us comprehend the distinctive understanding of the recipient of charity as a figure of Christ himself. Rather than thinking of the recipient as a
pro-entrepreneur or as a human to whom certain basic rights are owed, in
Christian charity the recipient is frequently spoken of as a conduit to salvation or, as just mentioned, standing in for Christ (Matt. 25:31–40).

While there are certainly complex historical and contemporary ideas intertwining with these forms of giving, I see attempts to collapse discussions of these various ethics of care into one another as erasing important distinctions in a way that makes it difficult to understand the actions taken by people and organizations.

Ethics

These questions about distinction and intertwining of ethics[7] bring us to the core of this book: understanding the ways these different ethicomoral assemblages—or the heterogeneous ways people understand and orient themselves toward something we might imperfectly call "the good" or "the right"—come together in collision, collaboration, coexistence, and compromise.[8]

In thinking through these situations, I draw on an existing tradition of Africanist anthropology that has sought to understand how various groups of Africans and Europeans have negotiated what Thomas O. Beidelman (1986), and subsequently Julie Livingston, called the moral imagination, or "the way we envision possibilities for a morally better or worse world than the one in which we live" (Livingston 2005, 19). In her work on debility in Botswana, Livingston called attention to how debilitating illnesses inspired such imaginative moments by highlighting our universal need for care and our need to explain and understand the social and personal crises that befall us (Livingston 2005). Such concerns are also at stake here as I seek to understand how people envision their relationships with, and responsibilities toward, orphans and other children whose lives raise similar questions of care and crisis. Through his research in Buganda, Mikael Karlström (2004) has also argued that an anthropology of ethics might help counterbalance the focus on the occult in anthropology by demonstrating the role that *kwabya lumbe* (last funeral rites) and the restoration of the kingship in Buganda have played in helping people productively resolve the sense of moral crisis that reigned in Uganda in the 1920s and again in the 1990s.

In addition to unraveling the ways history and social memory shape people's understanding of "the good," I am also interested in articulating the practices people engage in as they attempt to mold themselves and one another into particular sorts of ethicomoral subjects, or what Foucault (1990b) called "forms of subjectivation." To understand the sets of techniques that people use to align themselves with the ethics of sustainable development and charity, I draw on Foucault's later work to recognize how people use equipment (concrete institutions, technologies, and practices) as they try to transform a *logos* (a discourse that one believes states the truth and describes what one must do) into an *ethos* (an action-oriented matrix deeply embedded in the subject) that enables the *logoi* to be effortlessly deployed in the difficult moments of daily life (Foucault 2005; see Rabinow 2003). My analysis of the ethicomoral equipment used by development professionals and nuns in their practice of sustainable development and charity centers on an ethics of audit in the case of sustainable development and an ethics of virtue in the case of charity.

In combining my interest in the interactions between multiple ethical assemblages with an exploration of the ways people work on themselves to take up these distinctive ethics, I hope to provide a comprehensive description of these conflicting assemblages. I also hope to show how two contrasting modes of ensuring accountability—audit and virtue—shape both the subjectivity and the concrete actions that can be taken within each ethical assemblage.

Method

By describing charity, sustainable development, and Kiganda ethics of interdependence as assemblages that can be distinguished in such a way that they can then be put back into relation to one another, I engage in something of a thought experiment. As will become clear through the history and ethnography presented in this book, these three assemblages inform, influence, and conflict with one another, yet each is also apparent in the past and present articulations of the others. To speak of them as separable entities requires thinking of them as ideal types and acknowledging the active role the researcher plays in constructing the categories of analysis, while at the same time acknowledging a relation between the construct and reality (Weber 1904).

In constructing my analysis of these three ideal types, I draw on thirteen months of fieldwork conducted in Uganda in 2007–8 and 2010 and follow-up fieldwork with donor organizations in the United States and Europe in 2008 and 2010. Uganda has been central to both the history of Catholicism in Africa and the emergence of sustainable participatory development. Most of my fieldwork dealt with the daily practices of people living and working "on the ground" at village-level NGO field offices and charitable institutions. In addition, I draw on documents and interviews with more distant actors to demonstrate how these modes of defining and fulfilling obligations are linked to expansive global imaginaries, practices, and networks of people.

My time in Uganda was split between villages in two districts that lie immediately adjacent to Kampala, the capital city, and that are contained within the kingdom of Buganda. Most of those living in this area are Luganda-speaking people who identify as Baganda. The Baganda are the largest ethnic group, accounting for nearly 17 percent of the thirty-two million people living in Uganda (Uganda Bureau of Statistics 2002).

Both of these villages lie within the central region of Uganda, which was at the center of both the AIDS epidemic and the civil war that brought to power the current president, Yoweri Museveni. This region subsequently became a center for NGOs. As communities worked to rebuild and to cope with the deaths of hundreds of thousands of people, many of them parents, a number of NGOs established offices there. Many continue to work in this area, which has the benefit of being a commutable hour outside Kampala by public taxi. This region is at present experiencing a period of peace[9] and a 70 percent decline in HIV cases since the 1990s (Stoneburner and Low-Beer 2004). Nonetheless, its history of war, AIDS, and NGO intervention continues to shape the lives of the people who live there and the stories that others tell about them.

Hope Child

My analysis of the daily practice of sustainable development is based on a case study of Hope Child, a midsize indigenous NGO that was founded in 1995 by a Ugandan woman with experience as a child-welfare officer and as the director of an international Christian child-welfare NGO. Expanding from its original aim of operating the only toll-free child helpline in Uganda, Hope Child's programs are now shaped by a commitment to the holistic development of children and their caregivers and to the promotion of children's rights.

In 2007–8, the field office where I spent most of my time was implementing a multipronged program designed to strengthen grandparents caring for their young grandchildren, to establish Early Childhood Development centers, and to empower children and teenagers by establishing children's rights clubs. Hope Child's commitment to sustainable development and its attempts to avoid creating a population of dependent beneficiaries are especially striking given that it works with one of the few populations often thought to be appropriately dependent: children.[10] Yet by framing the children's grandparents or other guardians as the program's beneficiaries, its staff members moved away from positioning themselves as "child savers," a role they enthusiastically assumed during their early years of operating the child helpline, and toward empowering local adults the children can depend on while also emphasizing that the children have rights independent of their caretakers.

Since 2002, Hope Child has been increasingly successful in securing grants from a wide range of international foundations and governments. When I first visited Hope Child in July 2007, I was impressed by the staff's comprehensive, community-based approach to orphan support. I saw their success in securing funding from a broad range of international donors as evidence of their alignment with contemporary trends in orphan support programming, as well as proof of their effectiveness and integrity. I was not interested in writing an exposé of an ineffective or a poorly managed program, so I sought out Hope Child as an example of "best practices" within the field of orphan support and sustainable development. Using its donors' evaluations as a guide, I maintain that Hope Child is an exemplary case of the sustainable development assemblage at work and that the problems encountered were not products of incompetence or error but rather the outcomes of the sustainable development model.

Mercy House

My investigation of charity centers on the daily operations of Mercy House, a Catholic charity home for orphans, children and young adults with disabilities, and the elderly, run by the order of the Franciscan Sisters of Africa, which is made up of nuns from Uganda, Kenya, and Tanzania. Mercy House was founded in 1928 in a rural village two hours outside Kampala. During my fieldwork, Mercy House was home to nearly 150 residents. Rather than concentrating on a single population, the East African sisters running Mercy House have continued to open the gates to a broad range of people they see as needing care and support. This group includes orphans, children who have been abused, children and young adults with mental and physical disabilities, and elderly refugees and migrants who can no longer support themselves. Most of the children attend local schools, most of them also run by the Franciscan Sisters of Africa. For the Catholic nuns who run Mercy House, charity is a form of prayer and a way of reciprocating what they see as God's unmatchable gifts of love and grace.

———————————————

Both Mercy House and Hope Child alternately privilege the ethical assemblages of charity and sustainable development, and in neither case is a single assemblage exclusively in play. Rather, through both case studies I show how people shift between these ethics, struggling to justify their actions to themselves and others. In addition, it would be a mistake to think about these ethics through a binary distinction between the religious and the secular, since many of Hope Child's employees and volunteers are also practicing Christians, and each workday at the head office began with an hour of prayer, Bible study, testimony, and praise songs. And should we be tempted to think that perhaps sustainable development and charity can be thought of in terms of denominational distinctions, we need only look to the many secular and Protestant groups engaged in practices like those of the nuns of Mercy House, on one hand, and Catholic Relief Services'[11] embrace of microfinance, on the other, to realize that these ethical assemblages cannot be seen as strictly limited to a particular set of religious beliefs.

Nongovernmental Organizations

Hope Child and Mercy House are situated within a larger context of NGOs in Uganda. National and international NGOs have had a strong presence there since 1986, owing to the government's encouragement of civil society organizations after the civil war ended (Dicklitch 1998; Bornstein, Wallace, and Chapman 2006). Museveni's government was also unique in encouraging a climate of open discussion and engagement early in the AIDS epidemic. This not only led to an impressive decline in the number of AIDS cases, but also spawned a plethora of small-scale community-based organizations that focused on AIDS and served the widows and orphans left in its wake (Hunter 2003; Epstein 2007). By 1999 there were 3,500 aid organizations registered in Uganda, and they employed approximately 10 percent of the nonagricultural workforce. By 2009 there were nearly 8,000 registered NGOs (Uganda National NGO Forum 2009).

The proliferation of NGOs in Uganda during the last decades of the twentieth century parallels developments in other African nations that found their governments' ability to provide services sharply limited by the austerity measures imposed in the wake of the oil price–induced debt crisis of the 1970s, as I discuss in chapter 2. In addition to aligning with the shift away from the state provision of services, NGOs appealed to the two dominant camps of development critics: those who saw development as an essentially positive end hindered by flawed means, and those who saw more fundamental failings in the model of endless growth. For the former, NGOs provided a way to improve the development process by eliminating inefficiencies and expanding opportunities for participation and buy-in. For the latter, it seemed that NGOs might create a space for radical alternatives to the dominant models for development (Fisher 1997).

The dominance of NGOs in Uganda can also be contrasted with a minority of countries in Africa where the state manifests itself more tangibly in the lives of its people. In Botswana, NGOs complement materially significant state activities, including a robust national health care system and cash grants to families fostering orphans (Dahl 2009; Brada 2011). In Uganda, the state provides no such assistance to foster families. It does provide subsidized medical care and primary education, but the limited funding available after structural adjustment programs were imposed, combined with high levels of corruption, means these services are often of such low quality that they are popularly decried as useless. Such complaints not only were formally registered in Uganda's relatively free press during 2007–8 but were made privately through repeated jokes, including the one that transforms the government's Universal Primary Education slogan *bonna basome* (that all may study) into *bonna bakone* (that all may become idiots). In light of this view of government services, many Ugandans turn to NGOs and private for-profit institutions for health care and education services.

As faith-based NGOs, Hope Child and Mercy House are also part of an international trend toward faith-based provision of humanitarian and development aid and involvement of faith-based organizations in advocacy work (Ferris 2005). Yet despite the growth of such NGOs, the increasing demands for financial accountability have led many international faith-based NGOs to develop partnerships with local NGOs (secular or religious) instead of distributing aid through local churches as they had done in the past. Given the greater professionalism of NGOs, a long tradition of interchurch assistance is being replaced by a professionalized NGO sector (Ferris 2005), and quotidian forms of material giving are increasingly deemed problematic for a broad range of reasons (Halvorson 2012).

Christianity

Historians and anthropologists have long sought to understand the way that missionary encounters have affected people's lives, with many focusing on how missionaries paved the way, intentionally or not, for a mercantile economy by nurturing desires for imported products necessary for proper Christian living, such as soap and fabric[12] (Comaroff and Comaroff 1991). Recently anthropologists have also begun to pay serious attention to the experiences and beliefs of contemporary Christians in Africa and elsewhere. This delayed inclusion of Christian communities as objects of anthropological analysis can be attributed both to their being simultaneously too similar to and too different from the anthropologists and to their holding political views that made them "repugnant others" who should be avoided (Harding 2000; Robbins 2004; Bialecki, Haynes, and Robbins 2008).

In the past decade, this near-total absence in anthropology of attention to contemporary Christianity has been replaced by a number of ethnographic attempts to understand Christian practice on its own terms. Most of these studies have addressed the dramatic rise of Pentecostalism and other forms of charismatic Christianity (Hackett 1995; Gifford 1998; Maxwell 1998; Meyer 1999; Coleman 2000; Harding 2000; Robbins 2004; Marshall 2009; Cole 2010; Piot 2010; Haynes 2012a, Haynes 2012a, 2012b; Luhrmann 2012; O'Neill 2010). This book provides a contrast to these studies in that it focuses on contemporary Roman Catholicism.[13] Mainline churches, both Catholic and Anglican, continue to be a major presence in Uganda. In 2002, according to the estimates of Uganda's Bureau of Statistics, 42 percent of Ugandans were Catholic, 36 percent were Anglican, 5 percent were Pentecostal, 12 percent were Muslim, 4 percent practiced other religions, and 1 percent claimed to have no religious beliefs (Uganda Bureau of Statistics 2002).

Notwithstanding the introduction of more charismatic[14] forms of Catholicism and changes that the Second Vatican Council (1962–65) made to the liturgy and to the daily lives of priests, monks, and nuns, the religious lives of many Catholic Ugandans remain ordered by weekly attendance at mass, formal prayers that are often said aloud by families kneeling together before retiring, and rosary circles (which are seldom part of contemporary Catholicism in the United States and Europe). I mention these formal prayers and rosary groups not for their own sake, but as indexes to Ugandan Catholics' continued attachment to the forms of Catholicism introduced at the turn of the twentieth century.

Considering the nightly prayers that fill postcolonial living rooms raises questions about authenticity and contemporary Christianity's relation to colonial and missionary power. While earlier work on the anthropology of Christianity sought to explain conversion by looking at how Christianity provided converts with material or political advantages or enabled them to make sense of the rapidly changing social situations, these explanations make it difficult to see the actions and beliefs of Christians on their own terms and to understand the radical discontinuities that may accompany conversion (Robbins 2004). Instead of thinking about religion as something

Ugandans opportunistically employ to achieve existing, often material, ends, I find that Joel Robbins's (2007) discussion of conversion as a fundamentally transformative process through which people make sense of Christianity in terms of their own values, while also coming to value it on its own terms, more accurately describes the depth of religious practice that I found. And so while it is important to reflect on the colonial origins of Christianity in Uganda, it would be a mistake to see its contemporary practice as a veneer, as an import, or as belonging to anyone but Ugandans themselves.

What Lies Ahead

Since the end of the 1990s, the push for sustainable development has proceeded largely unquestioned. Through its polysemic potential, the term "sustainable development" has easily drawn a wide spectrum of supporters and is gaining strength as something of an absolute good. This book provides an extended critique of this approach by engaging with a larger set of conversations within the historical and anthropological literatures, which have sought to articulate how power, love, care, and dependence relate to one another across a range of African contexts. In this sense, my work continues a long tradition of anthropological critiques of development. Like those who have written of the more and less well-intentioned actors who have worked to change cultures, economies, and lives, I describe the myriad ways that Western models of development get it wrong, even when carried out by nationals under the sign of community ownership. Like other recent works, I argue that attempts to liberate are perhaps as much to blame as attempts to subjugate (Rose 1999). Yet in my efforts to think about the relation between sustainable development's self-defined opposite, charity, and Kiganda ethics of care, this book pushes past a clear denunciation of international philanthropy toward a more nuanced picture of how the ethics of gifts, dependence, and inequality are understood from within particular ethicomoral frameworks.

The chapters that follow explore the relations between charity, sustainable development, and Kiganda ethics of interdependence. In the first half of the book, I describe the norms, techniques, practices, and modes of reasoning involved in each of these divergent ethical assemblages. I address the normative value assigned to dependence and asymmetric forms of gift exchange within each of these assemblages and the ways these divergent valuations affect their interactions. In the second half, I look at the forms of subjectivation through which these visions of good become part of people's ethicomoral frameworks. Focusing on the differences between the ethics of audit and the ethics of virtue, I explore how these alternative modes of subjectivation influence programmatic decision-making.

Chapter 2 traces the genealogies of the three ethical assemblages at stake in contemporary conflicts over various approaches to the care of orphans in contemporary Uganda: sustainable development, charity, and Kiganda ethics of interdependence shaped both by an ethics of patronage and by *omutima omuyambi* (an indigenous virtue often described as an inborn "heart for helping"). For each assemblage, I weigh the moral valence assigned to questions of dependence and gift. By doing so, I provide the necessary historical context and reveal the temporal depth of the contemporary conflicts discussed throughout this book.

In chapter 3, I describe how Hope Child staff members drew on elements of the sustainable development assemblage in designing and implementing a program meant to strengthen grandparents caring for orphans. The first half of the chapter focuses on Hope Child's move away from making material donations to individual households. In place of these material gifts, it concentrated on community education events and the establishment of Early Childhood Development centers and grandparent support groups. I argue that while these changes were made in the name of increasing "community ownership" of the project, the staff's public commitment to community ownership paradoxically prevented them from listening to some of the community's most adamant demands. In the second half of the chapter, I argue that this focus on a certain variety of NGO-inspired participation and a priori assumptions about the categories of people most in need also excluded the poorest children and families from programs run by Hope Child and other NGOs in the area.

Chapter 4 explores the interplay between Kiganda ethics and Catholic charity, concentrating on the daily operation of Mercy House. My fieldwork at Mercy House revealed the contours of a specific contemporary assemblage that has coalesced in the interplay between Kiganda ethics and the vestiges of older forms of Catholic charity, which differ from contemporary Catholic social teaching. I claim that many people writing about charity hesitate to recognize the productive potential of charity because of their discomfort with inequality, dependence, and the coexistence of care and power.

Chapters 5 and 6 engage the emerging literature on the anthropology of ethics and examine the techniques for ensuring accountability that each of these ethical assemblages entails.

In chapter 5, I describe the increasing importance of audits aimed at improving transparency and cost-effectiveness in international development. I argue that the rise of the audit and other monitoring and evaluation practices not only has altered the ways that NGOs operate but has also changed the ways that development workers understand accountability and the role their mastery of audit technologies may play in their efforts to determine their own futures.

Chapter 6 contrasts the ethics of audit with how the nuns who run Mercy House use techniques of narrative and mimesis to shape themselves into subjects detached from worldly concerns, and how they learn to trust in, and make themselves accountable to, a divine, not an earthly, auditor. At the close of this chapter, I move toward a meditation on hope, human agency, and the temporal forms relevant to charity and sustainable development. I argue that the sisters of Mercy House see their work not through an agent-centered lens of developmental time oriented toward an earthly future, but rather focus on the immediate and eternal good accomplished through their cooperation with divine Providence.

In the concluding chapter, I take up these questions of action and agency to consider the political stakes of charity and sustainable development and the paths a reader might choose to take in responding to this book, ultimately asking what it might mean to consider engaging with human suffering in a way that makes us vulnerable to the demands we might face if not protected by walls both real and imagined.

TWO

Genealogies: Accidental Histories of Charity, Sustainable Development, and Kiganda Ethics of Interdependence

Throughout Uganda's history, colonists, missionaries, and aid workers have exchanged gifts, loans, and contracts with people without fully recognizing the nuances of the moral economies they were becoming involved in. In this chapter I trace three genealogies, examining how a diverse set of actors have approached dependence and gift giving. In doing so I follow Michel Foucault's genealogical method. Beginning with *Discipline and Punish* (1978), Foucault shifted away from looking for the underlying structures that determined the possibilities for thought, a method he termed "archaeology," toward a method he termed "genealogy." Foucault defined "genealogy" in opposition to the search for origins or predetermined forms. Instead, to help us step back and reconsider things we take for granted in the present, genealogy is meant to "identify the accidents, the minute deviations—or conversely, the complete reversals—the errors, the false appraisals, and the faulty calculations that gave birth to those things that continue to exist and have value for us" (Foucault 1984, 81). Whereas Foucault's archaeology looks to subconscious rules, his genealogical method centers on accidents and errors and takes seriously what actors tell us about what they do and why they do it.

Given the differences between these three assemblages—charity, sustainable development, and Kiganda ethics of independence—the genealogical task of tracing their construction requires a wide range of sources operating at different scales of analysis. While some of these mirror the sources Foucault used in his own genealogical work, others are quite different. In the first case I read my own ethnographic data in relation to other sources based on ethnography, comparative linguistics, archaeology, and archival analysis to construct a history of precolonial Buganda. Given the extensive historical research done on the social history of charity in Europe and missions in Buganda, I draw primarily on these secondary histories in describing the genealogy of charity. The array of institutional documents produced by the architects of sustainable development allows for an analysis of documents similar to those reflected in Foucault's own genealogical works. Secondary sources, such as Sebastian Mallaby's 2004 biography of James Wolfensohn, president of the World Bank from 1995 to 2005, reveal the contingency of this now-dominant development framework.

Ethics and Interdependence in Buganda

To understand the reaction to and impact of sustainable development and charity in Buganda, first we need to understand more fully the Kiganda ethics of interdependence they are interacting with. Yet in trying to explore the ideal typical assemblages of charity and sustainable development in relation to something my Baganda interlocutors described as their "tradition," we are left to balance the social fact of these statements and what they mean to those who make them against arguments that one cannot glean an accurate precolonial history from texts constructed by, or at the behest of, interested colonists, missionaries, and local elites (Hobsbawm and Ranger 1982). This is particularly true for a tradition that may be read as serving the interests of a small elite (Mamdani 1976). At one level it is enough to treat these statements as social facts that matter to those who make them and that help to order the contemporary moral frameworks in Buganda, while recognizing them as interested claims made for particular contemporary aims (Moore 1994). At a second level we must also recognize that statements about tradition are shot through with the ethics of Christianity, colonialism, and development, owing either to the interests of those who interpreted these statements or to the mixing of these forms in the minds of the Baganda themselves. At a third level, despite the problems of interpreting precolonial history in Africa, I am hesitant to ignore all that has been written on the history of hierarchy and dependence in precolonial Buganda. This is especially true given the writings of Holly Hanson (2003) and David Schoenbrun (1998). Both Hanson and Schoenbrun use a variety of innovative methods to make considerable strides toward a more grounded and nuanced analysis of precolonial Kiganda history. It is with these caveats that I proceed.

Having People

The works of historians like Hanson and Schoenbrun are linked not only methodologically but also conceptually to the work of Jan Vansina (1990) in their attention to the ways people have sought to transform material wealth into wealth in people. As I noted in the introduction, numerous scholars of Africa have described how people with even minimal resources often take on dependents to gain access to labor (Miller 1988), knowledge (Guyer and Belinga 1995), power, or social status by accumulating "wealth in people."

Igor Kopytoff and Suzanne Miers (1977) first used the term "wealth in people" in relation to the idea of "rights in people" in describing the demand for dependents of all kinds in precolonial Africa. Since their original usage, "wealth in people" has taken on a life of its own, given its analytic purchase in places where "interpersonal dependents of all kinds—wives, children, clients and slaves—were valued, sought and paid for at considerable expense in material terms" (Guyer and Belinga 1995, 92). In such circumstances, scholars have found that "wealth in goods" is "converted into followers" as often as possible (Vansina 1990). Subsequent elaborations have focused on the ways people are simultaneously patrons and dependents, receiving from those above them and giving to those below them, taking their positions in long hierarchical chains of support (Chabal and Daloz 1999; Swidler and Watkins 2007; Ferguson 2013; Haynes 2012a, 2012b).

In addition, even as patrons stand to gain from recruiting and maintaining dependents, they are also under a certain obligation to take on clients. Metaphorically speaking, one can be either a "feeder of people" or an "eater of people" (Bayart 1989). Redistribution thus becomes a moral imperative, and those who find themselves unable to "feed others" risk being accused of a moral failing (Moore 1994). In their work on transactional sex in rural Malawi, Ann Swidler and Susan Watkins (2007) stress the ethical imperative to take on dependents, writing that "redistribution is not only strategic and instrumental, it is also the moral thing to do" (151). This understanding of patronage as a moral obligation begins to break down modern distinctions between self-interest and altruism, in that one stands to gain some combination of material, symbolic, or spiritual capital by taking on dependents, while such an action is simultaneously thought to be an act of altruism, which is at times obligatory.

Assembling Patronage Networks

The emergence of patron-client hierarchies in Buganda has been traced to the introduction of banana permaculture early in the second millennium[1]

(Schoenbrun 1998). Hanson argues that the permanency of a banana garden made the gift of land a means for establishing a durable, productive, and highly visible relationship between *bakungu* (chiefs, those who gather up or assemble; sing. *mukungu*) and their followers. *Bakungu* were able to establish their power by recruiting people to live on their land. The abundance of land and its variable suitability for banana cultivation led to a situation throughout the precolonial period in which numerous *bakungu* actively competed for followers, who could be motivated to move either because of poor treatment by a *mukungu* or because of suboptimal fertility of a *mukungu*'s land. While the *bakungu* maintained the right to evict followers, this rarely happened; the relative security of those settlers provides a striking contrast to the precarious position of people in dependent relationships today (Hanson 2003).

Hanson also attributes the emergence of *butaka* (land held by clan leaders) to the stability of the banana gardens. As people were able to bury their dead on land they could inhabit for a long time, they began to attribute growing importance to tombs and to ancestors, who were increasingly seen as involved with the day-to-day affairs of their living relatives. These tombs gradually became the means of creating ancestral *butaka* land, which belonged to members of the clans. Although *butaka* belonged to the members of an ancestral clan, not all clan members lived on that land, and people belonging to other clans might be asked to settle there. Clan leaders (*bataka*) were charged with ruling everyone who settled on the land and with attending to clan members dispersed across the kingdom (Hanson 2003).

Sometime after 1200, a new form of kingship was introduced in Buganda: centralized power, an idea most likely imported from Bunyoro. Over time kings, who became known as *basekabaka* (sing. *kabaka*) about 1600, worked to consolidate their power against the authority of other chiefs and clan leaders (Schoenbrun 1998). Over the next three centuries, the *basekabaka* introduced new forms of authority that expanded the number and variety of people who had the ability to establish relationships through the gift of land. The first of these groups were the *balangira* (sing. *mulangira*), the princes who were the sons or grandsons of the *kabaka*. All these men were eligible to succeed the *kabaka* and were thus kept at some distance from the court to discourage coups. The second group were the *bami* (sing. *mwami*), men to whom the *kabaka* granted positions of authority as *bakungu* (territorial chiefs; sing. *mukungu*) or *batongole* (officers; sing. *mutongole*) based on the king's judgment of their achievements and abilities.

Over time the various chiefs appointed by the *kabaka* began to assume an authority greater than that of the *bataka* (clan leaders). In addition, the *kabaka* began to involve himself in selecting the *bataka* themselves.

All four types of leaders—princes, officers, territorial chiefs, and clan leaders—sought to establish relationships with the *bakopi*, the undistinguished commoners who needed to attach themselves to a territorial chief to secure access to land. The frequent translation of this word as "peasant" is somewhat misleading, since most male *bakopi* were not involved in subsistence agriculture, work that is still performed nearly exclusively by women. Male *bakopi* generally produced bark cloth and banana beer, hunted and fished, and served their *mukungu* in battle or in local maintenance projects. Chiefs sought to increase their dependent followers so as to raise their prestige and to signal the legitimacy of their authority (Hanson 2003). In addition to more diffuse forms of prestige, a chief could have his followers fight, maintain his compound, and render *busulu* (in-kind tribute), specifically bark cloth and home-brewed banana beer. In turn, followers stood to gain spoils of war, feasts, and land where their wives could grow food for the family. Followers were not asked to do agricultural labor for the chief, and they were more or less free to carry on domestic agriculture as they wished. Followers also hoped these relationships might lead to gifts passed down from the *kabaka* through the chiefs and possibly to places for their children in the *kabaka*'s court (Wrigley 1964, 21). Chiefs especially wanted followers who exhibited the virtues of *bwesige* (loyalty) and *buwulize* (obedience), while followers sought chiefs who demonstrated *ow'ekisa* (kindness) and who were *ayagalibwa abantu aba waggulu* (favored by their superiors).

While there is no single word in Luganda that encompasses the concept of patronage, the verbs that animate relationships between chiefs and their followers, such as *okusenga* (to join a chief) and *okusenguka* (to leave a chief), are significant in that they indicate followers' actions. This linguistic emphasis on clients' agency also shows the dynamic tension between dependence and social mobility in Kiganda patron-client relationships. Many Baganda men received large tracts of land from the *kabaka* in recognition of their prowess in battle, giving them the opportunity to acquire dependents of their own. Boys sent by their fathers' chiefs to serve as pages in the *kabaka*'s court could distinguish themselves through service, and many chiefs began their political careers this way. The importance of social mobility to the Baganda, and the role asymmetric dependence played in accomplishing that goal, can be seen in the proverb *Omuddu awulira y'atabaza engule ya mukama we* (the obedient servant carries his master's crown into battle), which is understood figuratively to mean that faithful service will be rewarded with wealth and glory (Fallers 1964).

The Entrenchment of Power and the Devaluation of Clients

Since the eighteenth century, this elaborate network of hierarchical ties has been subjected to events that have profoundly destabilized it. Although many of these events are associated with the colonial period, the alteration of these networks began more than a century before the British arrived.

During the eighteenth and nineteenth centuries, the Baganda aggressively tried to expand their kingdom, moving out from the area surrounding the contemporary capital of Kampala southwest along the shores of Lake Victoria. As the kingdom expanded, the *kabaka* appointed an increasing number of *batongole* chiefs, many of whom were given control over groups of people, including unfree laborers captured from neighboring groups, who were forced to work in *ebitongole* (labor parties). The rise in slave labor gradually made patrons less dependent on their clients for labor and other service, and physical force came to replace reciprocal obligation as the primary means of control (Hanson 2003).

Beginning in the early 1800s, the rise of external relations with Muslim traders from Zanzibar and the East African coast also changed the balance of power within the kingdom by increasing the demand for ivory and slaves, which could be exchanged for cloth and other goods. This in turn increased the status and wealth of the militia. Raiding had long been important in Uganda, and in the nineteenth century the army became even more central to the structure of Buganda, with a large number of commanders enjoying the privileges of high status (Wrigley 1964, 19). This standing militia was primarily engaged in wars of expansion and in capturing slaves and livestock from neighboring kingdoms, as it had been in previous centuries. Yet while the distribution of slaves had previously flowed through the hands of the *kabaka*, the rapid expansion of the kingdom and the slave trade created opportunities for chiefs to acquire slaves through other means, eventually decreasing the chiefs' dependence on the *kabaka*, resulting in a crisis of legitimacy (Hanson 2003).

The arrival of John Speke and James Grant at the court of Kabaka Mutesa I in 1862 marked the beginning of another strand in the transformation of hierarchical ties in Buganda. Initially the Baganda elite were eager to welcome the British and saw a possible relationship with them as aiding their ongoing attempts to expand their kingdom (Hanson 2003). In a series of letters to Colonel Charles George Gordon, Mutesa wrote of his desire for missionaries, gold, silver, iron, bronze, clothing, guns, cannons, and good houses.

While many Baganda saw the establishment of the protectorate as a patron-client relationship, the arrival of colonialism brought a series of changes that fundamentally altered the forms of mutual obligation developed since the turn of the second millennium. These changes were wrought through a series of colonial interventions that solidified and legitimized the positions of a "landed aristocracy" (Mamdani 1976) while simultaneously making clients less necessary, patrons more demanding, and class advancement more difficult. These interventions included the allotment of mailo land[2] to nearly four thousand chiefs, cash cropping, the emergence of a commodity-based elite culture, the introduction of formal schooling, the increasing stability of positions of political power, colonial demands on labor and resources made through indigenous authorities, and limits on people's ability to move. Thinking about this period of history requires acknowledging the ways indirect rule amplified and disseminated the authoritarian strands of Kiganda culture (Mamdani 1976) while understanding that it also undermined the legitimacy of hierarchical ties of interdependence.

When indirect rule was established and land was divided under the Uganda Agreement, signed in 1900 by the kingdom of Buganda and the British government protectorate, the Baganda elite attempted to regain some of the power they had lost when the British arrived (Hanson 2003). Perhaps most significant for this discussion was the allotment of 9,003 square miles of mailo land to some 3,945 chiefs of all ranks. While much of this land remained in the hands of chiefs who had held it before the 1900 agreement, the Uganda Agreement significantly altered the meaning of landownership. Before the agreement, chiefs appointed by the *kabaka* or other authorities held land at the pleasure of those who had given it to them. In addition, their ownership was inseparable from their jurisdiction over the people living on the land. With the introduction of the mailo system, land could be bought and sold, and landownership was ostensibly separated from political jurisdiction, fundamentally altering patron-client ties (Hanson 2003; Karlström 2004).

The introduction of small-scale cotton farming further altered how the land was used. Before this, land could be used only to produce subsistence food crops, to procure small in-kind rents, or to build relationships. After the introduction of cotton, landowners had the option of cotton farming, turning land once used to generate wealth in people into land that generated cash. This wealth was further converted into consumer goods that allowed chiefs to take up many of the cultural habits of the British, such as drinking tea, riding bicycles, speaking English, and living in brick houses with European-style furniture. These acquisitions created an elite culture that poor men wishing to join their ranks could no longer easily mimic (Fallers 1964).

The differential access to cash afforded to chiefs by their possession of land (which could be commercially farmed for personal gain) and by salaries paid by the colonial government, combined with the rise of a small number of elite boarding schools, let them further entrench their status. Select sons in Buganda had long been sent away to be educated in the courts of *kabaka* and senior chiefs in hopes of future advancement. While it was always more likely that the children of the elite would fill powerful posts, sons of peasants had also been sent to court for education, since there were always a number of positions to be filled. It cost nothing to send them. Some chiefs also feared that children who behaved badly would be killed and thus sought to keep their own children at home. The new Christian boarding schools were expensive and had limited availability, but they posed no bodily danger (Fallers 1964). The new opportunities for social mobility through careers in medicine, civil service, law, education, and religion were thus more likely to be taken up by elite sons, whose fathers could afford this Christian education. And while in some colonial contexts elites resisted conversion to Christianity, so that only those who failed to benefit from the earlier system attended Christian schools, the rapid conversion of most Baganda made this situation less relevant.[3]

In addition to the ways colonialism served to entrench the elite by the early twentieth century, the increasing demands patrons made on their clients on behalf of the British—in the form of hut tax, poll tax, and *kasanvu* (forced labor)—decreased the patrons' legitimacy and made clients less likely to respond to traditional requests for assistance. These restrictions severely limited clients' freedom of movement because people had to pay their poll tax and *busuulu* (rent) before moving to a new piece of land. Ultimately anyone leaving Buganda had to seek permission from the district chief (Hanson 2003, 186). In the traditional patronage system, people could easily leave their patrons, and their sense of agency was predicated on their choice of whom they would be dependent on. This mobility provided a crucial check on the power of patrons, who knew that they might be deserted if they mistreated their clients.

All these factors led to the alteration of the unequal, though mutually beneficial, relationships based on the obligations that structured the lives of the Baganda before the nineteenth century. Yet despite the ways the colonial period redefined the form and efficacy of patron-client ties in Buganda, positioning oneself in a hierarchy of patrons and clients remained an important and morally acceptable means of achieving social and economic security and advancement. Even today, being allotted school fees, jobs, contracts, or places on NGO participant rosters often depends on similar forms of patronage. Would-be dependents in contemporary Uganda seek out an array of patrons who can assist them. Given the limited nature of the support patrons provide and the uncertainty that shapes the lives of those living in Uganda and across sub-Saharan Africa, many choose to cultivate relationships of dependence and mutual obligation with more than one person who might be able to meet their needs. The multiplicity of these relationships not only is important given the variation and expansion of desired goods, services, and forms of protection, but also serves as insurance against the loss of patrons in a world that has become increasingly uncertain. In addition to the actual and perceived uncertainty of the present economy, the increasing market value of land in Uganda and the gradual shift toward a cash-based economy have made retaining clients even less attractive for many would-be patrons, who may now find it more beneficial to sell their land than to allow a client to farm it. Similarly, the high costs of schooling have made caring for children considerably more expensive, so that orphaned children are often able to find someone to provide lodging and food, but not school fees. This is particularly a problem for older children, who cannot take advantage of the government's Universal Primary Education program.

These contemporary issues have exacerbated the problems within the patronage system, which starting in nineteenth century made patrons less dependent on their clients while decreasing the clients' mobility. This situation has made other forms of care and redistribution increasingly important, and we now turn to one of these systems.

Having Heart

Interdependence—in the forms of reciprocal obligation, social security, and mobility—is joined in Buganda with a second ethics that is frequently articulated through the Luganda idiom of *mutima*,[4] or heart. In contemporary usage, the phrase *omutima omuyambi* is used to explain actions of kindness and generosity between kin and nonkin that exceed specific obligations.

Evarist Musumba, a retired civil servant whose family I lived with during the first three months of my fieldwork, defined this phrase, "A person with the heart for helping helps those he does not have an obligation to help." Musumba stressed that this form of help has become increasingly necessary given that rising costs have left many unable to care for the children who would traditionally have been their responsibility. Many people echoed the idea that assistance given out of *mutima* differs from other forms of assistance in its lack of obligation and reciprocity. Robert Sekamanya, the chairman of a village in Hope Child's catchment area, also defined *mutima* by its lack of reciprocity. "One can promise to pay fees for the children when they want to make the children dig for them. One can say, 'Let me help this child' while having an aim of cultivating his land. . . . We cannot call that 'real heart.' That is not helping." Sekamanya defined true *omutima omuyambi* as helping another without expecting to gain from the exchange. While givers can expect to be thanked for their efforts, people who act with the intention of benefiting concretely cannot be classified as motivated by "real heart."

As I spoke about *mutima* with Joan Nabagala, a woman caring for many children, she emphasized that it was impossible to persuade someone who does not have "the heart of sharing" to help people in need. Joan, who at that time was caring for six nieces and nephews in her home and paying the school fees for several others, said:

> Nobody has money these days, but if you have heart, the little you have you share. No matter how much money you have, if you don't have the heart of sharing you will not end up assisting anybody until the day of your grave. Some people say that I help because I have money, but for me I don't have money, but I do have that heart. . . . I can't tell you why I am assisting all of these children, it is just something about the way I was created.

For Joan, having a heart meant caring for the orphans in her family.

While it may sound as though she was simply fulfilling a set of kin-based obligations by caring for her deceased sister's children, within the patrilineal Kiganda kinship structure she had no such obligation because children officially belong to their father's clan. When children lose their mothers, they are not formally referred to as *abana bamulekwa* (orphans, the children left behind) until their fathers die, despite the difficulties they face. Joan conceived of caring for her sister's children not as an obligation but as something she did because she had been born with an inclination to help others.

In framing *mutima* as an inborn virtue that only a few people have, Joan's account presents this way of thinking as the opposite of the idea that a virtue like *mutima* can be inculcated through training or socialization (Laidlaw 2002; Mahmood 2004; Lester 2005). My Baganda neighbors insisted that it was not possible to learn *mutima*; it was something either you have or you don't. While many Kiganda virtues are thought to result from discipline or learning, this is not one of them.[5] The idea of *mutima* as an innate quality helps to account for why people seem to make little effort to alter others' *mutima*-governed decisions. People with *mutima* are frequently praised, but those without it are not openly chastised or encouraged to change.

During a conversation I had with Jjajja (Grandma) Teddy Kalibakate, who was caring for eight grandchildren and great-grandchildren, she said, "I would say that a person with heart has mercy. Someone could have lots of money, but they will not give you a coin. Yet the one with less money may decide to help." Jjajja Teddy was, I believe, referring to her daughter Scovia Nandugga, who, despite owning the most popular bar in the trading center, refused to help the family's numerous orphans, and to her son Ivan Musaazi, who owned a prosperous petrol station yet refused to pay school fees for any of his nieces or nephews. Under a logic of obligation, Scovia and Ivan might have been pressured to assist their sister Joan, quoted above, who was working in food service at an urban elementary school and paying school fees for most of the children in Jjajja Teddy's care. Yet under the logic of *mutima*, the problem was diagnosed as a difference of inborn qualities, which are not expected to change.

In my attempts to analyze this concept, I was confronted with a complex tangle. Ideas including patron-client reciprocity, a culture of "sharing" or generalized reciprocity, and claims that *mutima* has always been a Ugandan virtue were interspersed with Christian ideals of charity and mercy and the giver's relationship with God. One of the central arguments of this book concerns how Baganda women and men, acting within ethics of patronage and *mutima*, saw something recognizable in the forms of Christian charity that arrived with the British and French missionaries in the last quarter of the nineteenth century. Over the twentieth century, many Ugandans have so incorporated these understandings of charity into their own ethical assemblages that it is now difficult to ask about *mutima* without receiving an answer that simultaneously references ahistorical Kiganda values and Christian notions of charity.

The following chapters discuss these interactions in depth, but first I must work through a brief genealogy of Christian charity. In the next section I discuss the emergence of charity within Christian theology, outlining some of the criticisms raised since the seventeenth century, and show the role of charity in Christian missions in Uganda.

Charity

The Rise of Charity

The history of Christian charity, *caritas*, stretches back at least as far as the prophetic period of Israel, with the book of Deuteronomy instructing the people to give 10 percent of their income every three years in *tzedakah* (justice or charity) to those living within the settlement who had no hereditary right to the fruits of the community's labor (Deut. 14:22–27, 26:12).[6] In the book of Tobit, written centuries after Deuteronomy, *tzedakah* took on a very different meaning, with giving alms replacing offering sacrifice in the temple when distance prevented doing so in person (Tob. 1:6–8). In this redefinition, the hands of the poor became substitutes for the sacrificial altar (Anderson 2009).

The concept of alms as a substitute for sacrifice became both more central and more intense in the New Testament, in which the poor serve not as altars where sacrifices may be made but as figures of Christ himself. To give but one of many examples, consider Matthew's account of Jesus' teaching about the Last Judgment after the Second Coming of Christ:

> When the Son of man comes in his glory . . . he will separate them from one another, as a shepherd separates the sheep from the goats. . . . Then the king will say to those on his right, "Come, you who are blessed by my Father. Inherit the kingdom prepared for you from the foundation of world. For I was hungry and you gave me food, I was thirsty and you gave me drink, naked and you clothed me, ill and you cared for me, in prison and you visited me." Then the righteous will answer him and say, "Lord, when did we see you hungry and feed you, or thirsty and give you drink?" . . . And then the king will say to them in reply, "Amen, I say to you, whatever you did for one of these least brothers of mine, you did for me." (Matt. 25:31–40)

Here giving alms to the poor is not so much making a sacrifice as loving, and in some way caring for, God himself. In the writings of the apostle Paul, the emphasis on loving one's neighbor becomes even more pronounced as love of neighbor and love of God are fused, with love of one's neighbor becoming the very enactment of loving God (Taubes and Assmann 2004).

This "gospel of love and charity" eventually became crucial to the spread of Christianity across the Roman Empire. Historian Peter Brown (2002) has persuasively argued that from the fourth through the seventh century Christian bishops, with their lay helpers and clerics, redefined the masses of "noncitizens" in the ancient cities. Through their actions, they transformed the categories of difference by which people in late antiquity understood their position in society, moving from a world of citizens and noncitizens to a world of the rich and the poor. Bishops thus increased their own power by expanding the scope and necessity of activities proper to the "love of the poor." Brown argues that it was through these bishops that the nature of giving was gradually transformed during late antiquity from the wealthy person's striving to be a *philopatris*, a lover of his home city, to his desiring the status of a *philoptôchos*, a lover of the poor (Brown 2002).

Criticisms of Charity

Throughout the Middle Ages, the Catholic Church continued to be the primary institution providing services to those who were poor or in danger of becoming poor. Beginning with the Elizabethan Poor Law in 1601, periodic movements sought to replace religious charity with more secular forms of engaging with the poor. Many of these measures were based on the idea that the rich should help the poor in a manner that would discourage idleness while assisting morally upright people unable to care for themselves and their families. By the end of the eighteenth century, French proponents of the Enlightenment were advocating for eliminating Catholic charity in favor of programs oriented toward *bienfaisance*, referring to rational, methodical, state-driven relief aimed at eliminating both poverty and idleness. The advocates of *bienfaisance* argued that the charitable institutions of the ancien régime were more interested in their own spiritual well-being than in the material well-being of those who sought assistance through the hospitals and home relief programs. They also claimed that almsgiving failed to distinguish between the deserving and undeserving poor and therefore "aggravated the problem of poverty by licensing improvidence and sloth and discouraging enterprise" (Jones 1982, 3). This way of thinking was reinforced by Enlightenment philosophers such as Rousseau, who wrote, "Dependence on men since it is without order engenders all the vices and by it master and slave are mutually corrupted" ([1762] 1979, 85).

After the French Revolution, the Catholic Church struggled to rebuild itself, reasserting its opposition to the Enlightenment and renewing its commitment to charity and to international missionary efforts. In addition, the new forms of poverty that arose alongside industrial capitalism inspired a century of periodic papal encyclicals[7] discussing the ways the church and its members should respond to poverty, inequality, and injustice. The first of these encyclicals was *Rerum Novarum*, published by Pope Leo XIII in 1891. While still deeply conservative about the hierarchical ordering of the world, he used the idea of the common good to argue that people are inherently interdependent beings who are obliged to care for one another. Whereas later popes would emphasize egalitarian aims, Leo XIII took for granted the continued existence of social strata and focused on responsibilities to one's fellow humans given one's position in the social hierarchy (Catholic Church 1939). As I describe below, this focus on hierarchical redistribution resonated with understandings of patronly *mukisa* (kindness) already present in Uganda.

Mission and Charity in Uganda

Uganda is often cited as unique in mission history, given the speed of its conversion to both Catholic and Protestant forms of Christianity. As opposed to many other contexts where conversion occurred slowly, often beginning with marginalized people who could not succeed in traditional society, Christianity was readily embraced in Buganda, and many of its earliest converts were chiefs, pages, and other members of the king's court (Hastings 1995; Bevans and Schroeder 2004; Martin 2009).

The Church Missionary Society (CMS) sponsored the first group of missionaries to arrive in Uganda, in 1877.[8] In addition to evangelization, Protestant missionary societies, including the CMS, stressed the need for political, social, and economic development, putting the push for civilization and commerce nearly on a par with the push for Christianity. The protestant social gospel movement emphasized the need to bring about the kingdom of God using the tools of science and efficient planning. By the end of the nineteenth century, the mission revival reached fever pitch with nationalist ideas of manifest destiny. The missionaries came to see themselves as part of the special plans Providence had laid out for their assigned countries (Bevans and Schroeder 2004).

The White Fathers, an order of French Catholic missionaries founded in Algeria eleven years earlier by Cardinal Charles Lavigerie, arrived in Uganda in 1879 (Bevans and Schroeder 2004). The White Fathers were one of a number of religious orders created during the nineteenth century as the Catholic Church attempted to rebuild itself after the French Revolution. Despite their differing views on the Enlightenment and the role of the church hierarchy, French Catholic missionaries of this period shared the British Protestant missionaries' interest in training local clergy and lay catechists who could participate in the "evangelization of Africa by Africans" (Hastings 1995).

The presence of both Protestant and Catholic missionaries, added to Kabaka Mutesa's and later Kabaka Mwanga's attempts to recruit missionaries as political allies, laid the groundwork for two decades of civil war during which recent converts to Islam, Protestantism, and Catholicism fought for control of the kingdom. Many of these Christian converts were young pages of Mutesa's court, and many became the first lay leaders of the Catholic and Protestant churches in Uganda, often working in isolation from their European counterparts during the missionaries' periodic expulsions from the kingdom. Over the course of the 1880s and 1890s, Catholics, Protestants, and Muslims formed a series of shifting alliances with one another. By 1890 the Catholics, with the help of Kabaka Mwanga, and the Protestants, with the help of England, were battling for political and religious control of Buganda. In December 1890 the British East Africa Company sent Captain Frederick Lugard and one hundred men to end the fighting between the Catholic and Protestant factions in Buganda. However, the 450 guns that he distributed to the badly outnumbered Baganda Protestants for self-protection were interpreted as a declaration of war by the Baganda Catholics, who made a preemptive attack on the British. The machine-gun fire of Captain Lugard and his men met their advance, and the Catholics retreated to Buddu. Lugard attempted to establish a three-way sharing of power giving different Ugandan counties to the Protestants, Catholics, and Muslims, but this solution proved unsatisfactory to all parties, and both the Catholics and Protestants appealed to the British government. In 1893 Lugard left Uganda and was replaced by Sir Gerald Portal, who had been given the power to establish a British protectorate. In 1894 all the fighting factions signed the treaty establishing the protectorate. This civil war led by young Christian converts changed the stakes of their conversions, making them decide between Catholicism and Protestantism rather than between Christianity and traditional religion (Fallers 1964; Low 1971a; Kiwanuka 1972; Hastings 1995). The continuing significance of Protestant and Catholic identity in Uganda also helps explain why Pentecostal churches, which arrived in 1960, have had difficulty attracting church members away from the mainline denominations (Gifford 1998).

After the establishment of the British protectorate, the White Fathers decided the only way to rid Uganda of the misconception that all Protestants were British and all Catholics were French was to leave and ask British Catholic missionaries to take their place (Gale 1959). In 1895 the first group of Mill Hill Fathers arrived from Britain, and they were joined in 1906 by a group of six sisters, including Mother Mary Patrick,[9] who would go on to found the all-African order of the Franciscan Sisters of Africa (Louis 1964). During the first half of the twentieth century, the Catholic Mill Hill missionaries focused on catechesis and on providing charity through schools, hospitals, and orphanages.

Catholic social teaching's emphasis on hierarchy and on acts of material kindness within that hierarchy not only shaped the vision and strategies of Catholic missionaries in the nineteenth century but also found a lasting resonance with the Kiganda ethics of hierarchical interdependence described above. There is evidence that many Baganda found something similar to *mukisa* in the goods and services doled out by Catholic missionaries. In an 1899 letter complaining about local opposition to the fees charged at the Protestant Church Missionary Society's hospital, Anglican archdeacon Robert Henry Walker writes:

> The people are unreasoning and look at the whole question from the point of view of "kindness" and say that the R.C.s [Roman Catholics] are kinder. . . . [T]hey give all of their medicines away free of charge. . . . The more I see of these people the more I see that "kindness" is the one thing necessary in their eyes. (Hanson 2003, 20)

I am not implying that the Baganda and the Catholics were operating within the same logic, but there was an affinity between their actions, resulting from their distinct ethical frameworks, that allowed for certain moments of recognition. As I discuss in chapter 4, over the course of the twentieth century Christian charity and Kiganda ethics have become ever more deeply intertwined, starting with the rapid and widespread conversion to Christianity at the end of the nineteenth century and the gradual emergence of a large community of Ugandan clergy and catechists.

Vatican II

The Second Vatican Council (1962–65) opened debates concerning the best mode of improving the lives of the poor and the future of missionary activity. Vatican II centered on the idea that the essence of God's grace existed in all world religions, making people question the need for missionary activity. The independent African religious orders of nuns, monks, and priests that the missionaries left behind as support for the missions faded were deeply affected by the post–Vatican II critiques of their mission-ary endeavor, since they were largely cut off from the global flow of phil-anthropic capital. Catholics in Europe and the United States were leaving the church in large numbers, and those who stayed were less interested in supporting missionary work, since conversion now seemed now less neces-sary and charity work less than revolutionary. As the streams of money that had previously filled the coffers of missionary orders dried up, the religious orders could no longer support the African orders they had helped create. Many of the African sisters I spoke with noted the difficulties they had ex-perienced in the wake of Vatican II, when they suddenly found themselves without foreign support, yet they spoke of feeling freedom and pride after their separation from their European founding congregation.

The papal encyclicals on Catholic social teaching that came after Vat-ican II were markedly different from those written earlier in the century (Sniegocki 2009). Whereas in earlier times they were primarily oriented toward the solidarity and salvation that would be possible after the Sec-ond Coming of Christ, the writings of Pope John Paul II focused on the possibility of bringing about the City of God in worldly time. The goal of egalitarian solidarity in this world—plus attention to the part that science, technology, rational planning, and small civil society organizations play in attaining this goal—brings contemporary Catholic social teachings into relatively close alignment with mainstream approaches to development.

Yet, as will become clear in future chapters, there is a way the work under-taken by African sisters, such as the Franciscan Sisters of Africa, remains closer to the late nineteenth- and early twentieth-century forms of charity work. The Franciscan Sisters of Africa's commitment to charity not only puts them in an awkward position relative to the approaches to sustainable development but has also left them somewhat out of alignment with more progressive strands of the Catholic Church.

Sustainable Development

Sustainable development, which often defines itself as charity's opposite, is now among the most popular frameworks for thinking about how eco-nomic growth and alleviation of poverty can occur simultaneously. The term has many distinct, though perhaps not unrelated, meanings cur-rently in use in the academic and policy literatures (Homberg and Sand-brook 1992; Elliott 1999). Indeed, several authors have argued that it is in fact sustainable development's polysemic nature that has made it such an attractive concept (Redclift 1987; Mitchell 1998). It is possible, however, to group these definitions into two distinct categories, each with its own history and primary frame of reference. The first category concerns the environmental impact of development projects, and it is the one most often referred to in the primary and secondary literatures when the term "sustainable development" is used (Redclift 1987; Adams 1990; Homberg and Sandbrook 1992; Escobar 1995; Elliott 1999; Fernando 2003; Green and Chambers 2006; Baker 2006). Although it has its roots in the environmentalist movements of the 1960s and the early United Nations seminars held in 1971 and 1972 concerning the reconciliation between environmentalism and development (Adams 1990), the environmental definition of sustainable development was most prominently articulated in the 1987 United Nations report "Our Common Future," also known as the Brundtland Report. "Our Common Future" defined sustainable development as "development that meets the needs of the present without compromising the ability of future generations to meet their own needs" (World Commission on Environment and Development 1987). This understanding of sustainable development has been criticized by anthropologists and other scholars of development for reinventing nature as something to be managed (Escobar 1995), for emphasizing environmental degradation's effects on growth (Redclift 1987), and for being imprisoned within the market logic of capitalism (Fernando 2003; West 2006).

The second definition of sustainable development centers on the financial sustainability of development projects. When the development workers I studied at Hope Child ask about "sustainability" under this second definition, they are asking whether the project can continue to produce benefits beyond the life of the intervention. This was the only definition of sustainable development used by the development workers I encountered at Hope Child or at any of the other NGOs I visited during my fieldwork in Uganda. In light of this, I leave alone the literature on environmental sustainability and focus on financially sustainable development.

The history of this form of sustainable development comprises three related themes. The first concerns the tensions between concepts of aid, which posit it alternatively as a gift or as a loan. The second theme concerns the subject or target of developmental transformation, and the third concerns the form and scale of capital thought to be most effective for bringing about social transformation. Yet despite the variations that occur along these axes, the focus on transformation and on independence from ongoing aid remains consistent. In tracing this story, I pay particular attention to Uganda's experience at turning points in its development history, not only to give the historical context needed to understand the ethnographic data presented in later chapters, but also to show Uganda's unique role in creating models for sustainable development in the final decades of the twentieth century.

Assembling Sustainable Development

By the end of the 1970s, World Bank president Robert McNamara's "integrated rural development projects" were largely thought to have failed, and the bank was coming to be seen as overextended and bloated. In addition to these internal problems, developing countries' debt burdens were growing rapidly because of the dramatic decline in prices for raw commodities such as copper, coffee, and cocoa, and because of the oil crises of the 1970s. As commodity prices fell and oil prices shot up, countries took out large loans so they could buy the increasingly expensive petroleum products they needed to support their industrializing economies. In an effort to resolve the credit crisis, in 1979 the World Bank developed a series of policies and loan products aimed at opening markets and increasing foreign exchange. To secure these structural adjustment loans, countries trapped by the oil-induced debt crisis were required to radically devalue their currencies so they could increase their exports and thus repay the petrodollar loans. They were also required to cut public spending so as to reduce their dependence on foreign credit (Berg 1982). This shift in policies from promoting comprehensive development to lending that required dramatic cuts in public services heralded a new era at the World Bank. These measures also proved a good match for the global climate of support for the conservative policies introduced under the administrations of Ronald Reagan and Margaret Thatcher.

By the early 1990s the World Bank, and development institutions more generally, faced an increasing number of critics who argued that development had done little to help the world's poor. While some of these arguments were specifically related to the Structural Adjustment Programs, many arguments had been simmering for decades. Before moving forward with the ascendancy of sustainable development at the World Bank, it is important to pause and consider three critiques that led to the crisis in the development community in the 1990s.

As we saw earlier, arguments concerning the detrimental effects of dependence on charity can be traced back to the French Revolution. Yet in the 1960s a new variation on this theme emerged. Theodore Schultz's (1960) critique was one of the first to claim that food aid such as the United States PL480 programs, which purchased surplus crops from US farmers to be

donated or sold at reduced prices to developing countries, depressed local production and led to greater food dependence. Schultz argued that by
suppressing internal production, foreign aid made countries dependent on
imports. While this is not a claim we frequently associate with eighteenth-
and nineteenth-century opposition to outdoor relief and the construction
of poorhouses, in some ways Schultz's critique resonates with these earlier
readings of charity and with contemporary neoliberal manifestations of
sustainable development.

By the 1970s, a similar indictment of the harmful dependency relationships between rich and poor nations emerged. This school of thought was
based on Andre Gunder Frank's (1967) view that underdevelopment was
not a natural state but a product of the trade relationships between the
capitalist metropolis and its dependent satellites (Mamdani 1976; Cardoso
and Faletto 1979; Wallerstein 1979). In his influential *Capitalism and Underdevelopment in Latin America: Historical Studies of Chile and Brazil*, Frank
(1967) outlined the thesis that became central to the dependency theory
of underdevelopment. According to Frank, underdevelopment should be
thought of not as an ahistorical stage that naturally precedes development,
but rather as a state that results from capitalistic relationships between
the periphery and the core. Frank argued that poor countries would never
"catch up" because the well-being of those in the capitalist core depends
on the poverty of the exploited periphery (Frank 1967).

In addition to these critiques of dependency, during the early 1980s
there was growing concern that development projects often failed to consider the perspectives and insights of project beneficiaries. In *Rural Development: Putting the Last First*, Robert Chambers (1983) argued that development research undertaken by "outsiders" suffered from misleading data
derived through surveys and "development tourism" in which program
designers, evaluators, and funders make carefully orchestrated whistle-stop
tours of their project sites. He argued that development research is shaped
by more than just the biases toward the professional interests of those involved; it is also shaped by a series of biases that privilege the experiences
of relatively well-off people who live near main roads and have chosen
to participate in existing development projects. Chambers argued that research projects that did not reach the poorest of the poor were biased toward ineffective Western technological interventions and failed to integrate
the valuable knowledge rural people possess about their own problems
and possibilities (Chambers 1983).

Chambers proposed a series of participatory research methods that he
argued would include marginalized rural people in development research

and planning. The World Bank gradually embraced several of these methods during the late 1980s and early 1990s. The importance of including potential beneficiaries, particularly poor ones, in project decision-making and implementation was given formal recognition in the early 1990s.[10]

By 1994, at the World Bank's annual meeting, held in Madrid that year, protestors came together under the banner of the "Fifty Years Is Enough" campaign, a reference to the bank's fiftieth anniversary. The protestors cited the toll that structural adjustment programs had taken on the world's poor and the environmental disasters created by large-scale projects such as hydroelectric dams. The World Bank's critics pointed to more innovative approaches, including microfinance and participatory development, that were being implemented by NGOs, which they claimed had far greater success than the massive World Bank projects (Mallaby 2004).

When the energetic financial adviser and philanthropist James Wolfensohn was appointed by US president William (Bill) Clinton to lead the World Bank in 1995, he seized the chance to respond to the bank's many critics. Instead of defending the bank against the NGOs' accusations, he embraced them and joined in their critiques, vowing to return the bank to its poverty-fighting mission of the 1960s and 1970s. In his attempts to change the face of the World Bank and bring it closer to the "clients" it purportedly was established to serve, clients he alternately imagined as the national governments of poor countries and the poor citizens themselves, Wolfensohn took up the idea of participatory development in which both poor governments and poor citizens would play a much greater role in designing policies to reduce poverty (Mallaby 2004).

Wolfensohn was further convinced of the need to cede project ownership to governments and communities by two other ideas. The first was brought to his attention by World Bank anthropologist Scott Guggenheim, who argued that the bank's true clients were not national governments but the people of the countries those governments claimed to serve. Guggenheim had arrived in Indonesia in 1994, and his deep frustration with its corrupt government led him to speak publicly about the government's misuse of bank funds and to create the Kecamatan Development Project, in which small grants would be allocated directly to subdistrict councils to be spent on projects proposed, designed, and monitored by local villagers.[11] Guggenheim started his program in 1998, and in 2001 the World Bank took over the project, which came to account for half of its lending to Indonesia. The creation of the local institutions necessary to carry out an undertaking like the Kecamatan Development Project can be seen as a key example of the focus on "social capital," which in the late 1990s was beginning to replace the 1960s and 1970s focus on "human capital" (Mallaby 2004, 202–5).

The second inspiration for Wolfensohn's push toward participatory development came from Uganda. By 1997 Uganda had established itself as a model for international development. Through its use of a market-based agenda focused on reducing public spending and currency devaluation and further liberalizing the coffee market, combined with the first prolonged period of peace since its independence in 1962, President Yoweri Museveni and his finance minister Emmanuel Tumusiime-Mutebile proudly took credit for the 40 percent increase in the gross domestic product that the country had achieved since 1987 and for ending decades of civil war. Not insignificantly, Uganda was also stunningly successful in using community-based care organizations and in its own campaign to curb the transmission of HIV/AIDS during this same ten-year period (Epstein 2007). In light of these successes, international organizations began to look to Uganda as the place to find the answers to the problems of development. While some argued that it was Uganda's implementation of standard structural adjustment policies that had led to the remarkable growth rates, others used Uganda to demonstrate the success of other agendas, including debt relief, privatization, and decentralized government (Mallaby 2004).

Ultimately the strength and ability of Tumusiime-Mutebile, combined with the promise that Wolfensohn and World Bank East Africa director Jim Adams saw in participatory approaches to international development, determined what elements of Uganda's development success would be incorporated into their international program. Together Tumusiime-Mutebile and Adams succeeded in moving the meetings of the World Bank Consultative Group, in which Uganda's development strategies were discussed, from Paris to Kampala. They also worked together to develop the Participatory Poverty Plan in 1997 and the Participatory Poverty Assessment in 1998, in which thousands of specially hired staff were sent out to interview poor people across the country. Despite the fact that Uganda's poverty reduction was achieved before these interventions were implemented and that Uganda largely had followed the dogma of structural adjustment, the focus on process, on country ownership, and on popular participation were the elements of Uganda's development policies that were ultimately included in Wolfensohn's Comprehensive Development Framework (Mallaby 2004, 213–31).

Perhaps more important, "community-owned" development projects offered a solution to the problem of providing public goods after state-funded services were eliminated during the 1990s. Although he was a proponent of debt relief, Wolfensohn did not oppose structural adjust-ment and felt that many of the Ugandan policies had been economically wise. The problem with structural adjustment, in Wolfensohn's view, thus lay not at the core of the policies but rather in the way they were carried out without regard to their social costs. Community-owned development schemes provided one route out of this problem. The need to provide an inexpensive substitute for state-funded public goods eliminated under structural adjustment was among the primary forces that led other states and international financial institutions, such as the World Bank, to pro-mote sustainable development (Kremer and Miguel 2007).

This is evinced in documents such as *Beyond the Washington Consensus: Institutions Matter* (World Bank 1998). While the authors of this working paper, Shahid Javed Burki and Guillermo Perry, concluded that many of the structural adjustment measures in Latin America brought significant economic growth, they went on to argue that sustained growth would re-quire these countries to create "institutions," which they defined as the formal and informal rules that shape the behavior of individuals and or-ganizations. For example, in addressing the need to develop a robust edu-cational system, Burki and Perry advocated increasing parents' involvement in their children's schools. "One way of improving the performance of schools in the region is to provide greater participation to parents in the schools' management. Empowerment (or voice) then becomes a means to ensuring that the school acts according to the interests of the household" (World Bank 1998, 35). Burki and Perry largely attributed the success of educational reform in Chile to "local-level participation in the design of the education process, generating a sense of ownership within communi-ties" (100). The community management board thus became a plausible alternative to more costly government management, and the unexpected links between empowerment, community participation, and neoliberal-ism came more clearly into view (Cruikshank 1999; Dean 1999; Leve 2001; Hindness 2004; Gupta and Sharma 2006; Sharma 2006; Li 2007). Through these processes, community organizations are also transformed. They are no longer political organizations making demands of the government; rather, they are focused on solving their communities' problems without government assistance. Community groups thus became "dedicated to generating income, not expressing protest" (Paley 2001, 6).

This focus on comprehensive community-based strategies was part of the more general push toward development that would be sustainable. The idea of sustainability itself is not new; it has been part of develop-ment economics since its inception. The idea that a country will "take off"

(Rostow 1960) into its own industrialized orbit is not unlike the idea that a country should strive for sustainable development so it can someday stop depending on subsidized capital flows. Going back to an earlier discussion, colonial governments were advised to reduce their dependence on their home governments through taxes and forced labor, and Henry Venn, president of the Church Missionary Society from 1841 to 1872, outlined the need to found churches that were self-supporting, self-governing, and self-propagating (Baur 2001). And so the question becomes, What is new about sustainable development?

In studying both the history and the contemporary enactment of this ethics of engagement with the poor, there are two ways the sustainable development assemblage, which emerged in the late 1990s, differs from earlier considerations related to sustainability.

The first and more important of these is the double focus on participation and investment in local institutions as the key mechanisms for achieving sustainable development. No longer is physical capital or even human capital the key; now the key is the social capital found in "the community" and, especially, in "community organizations." Tania Li (2007) has highlighted the links between such international community development schemes and the ascendancy of what Nikolas Rose (1999) has termed "government through community" in Europe and the United States. Government through community does not act on an existing physical or social space but rather defines, maps, and empowers new networks of individual actors who are conceived of as imperfect and in need of management, yet capable of bringing about social and economic change. Efforts to perfect and make use of indigenous institutions and people in some ways reflect colonial strategies of indirect rule, but government through community places a greater emphasis on how emotion is used to tie individuals together and spur them to construct microcultural identities (Li 2007, 323–36; Rose 1999).

Second, before sustainable development took hold in the 1990s, nonsustainable financial contributions could be made. Now each action needs to be sustainable and infinitely replicable. Whereas in an earlier moment the World Bank needed to be self-sustaining, now every local community organization must be. In this movement the individual villager must now pay back the loan or be refused the gift, rather than leaving the burden of sustainability to an official in the national government.

In the coming chapters I follow the movements, conflicts, and convergences of the three assemblages—charity, sustainable development, and Kiganda ethics of interdependence—as they played out at Hope Child and Mercy House in 2007 and 2008. In exploring the ways that figures of dependence and gift giving influenced programmatic planning, personal moments of moral decision-making, and forms of ethical work, I walk a fine line so as to view Hope Child and Mercy House as ideal types of sustainable development and Christian charity while also showing the entanglements between the assemblages.

THREE

Waiting: The Disappointments of Sustainable Development

At lunch on the shaded veranda of a restaurant near the Sebanda sub-county trading center, my research assistant George Mpanga[1] and I chatted about his plans to send a grant proposal to the Rotary Club of Kampala. His brother wanted to do something for their hometown, and the Rotary Club was willing to fund projects provided they cost less than 10 million UGX (US$5,882),[2] would benefit the whole community, and would be sustainable.

George had initially proposed a subsidized medical dispensary or a school lunch program as priority needs for the town. He thought for a moment, then dismissed these ideas. "School lunch programs and medical dispensaries are good, but they're not sustainable." He then suggested that his brother might purchase a set of plastic chairs and a tent that could be used for workshops. I asked if these chairs were really needed. "No, not really," he replied. I asked, "What's the point of providing things that are sustainable and benefit the whole community but that people don't need?" George agreed that people could always sit on mats on the floor, but chairs were "sustainable," and this alone made them a good prospect for securing funding.

The primary aim of sustainable development is to create programs that will ultimately become self-sufficient. In line with this aim, development workers engaged in these projects are obliged to make program decisions that will empower local people while at all costs avoiding creating dependence. As shown in chapter 2, developing interventions that will outlast a specific program is at the center of the sustainable development assemblage. In discussions at Hope Child and the other NGOs operating in Sebanda subcounty, determining if an intervention is likely to yield long-term self-sustaining benefits is in many cases more important than determining what intervention might be most needed. From tiny decisions about what kinds of toys or play equipment could be provided to the Early Childhood Development (ECD) centers (locally made climbing structures and banana-fiber dolls are sustainable, manufactured soccer balls are not) to larger discussions about the payment of school fees, the "sustainability" of the intervention was the key term of the debate.

In this chapter I build on the discussion of the emergence of sustainable development laid out in chapter 2. I focus on the ways Hope Child, a Ugandan NGO that supports orphans and their caregivers, drew on elements of the sustainable development assemblage in designing and implementing its interventions. The short-term program funding and a more general opposition to interventions that might make people dependent on outside organizations meant that nonmaterial interventions, such as training or forming community groups, were highly preferable to material supports such as blankets or money for school fees, which were often glossed as "handouts." Where material support was given, it was generally not as goods but as one-time capital-intensive projects, which would presumably outlive the program staff's involvement, or as microloans. Avoiding nonmaterial programming was also considered preferable in a climate where donor organizations were asking NGOs to reach an ever-increasing number of clients with holistic, multifaceted programs.

The first half of this chapter focuses on Hope Child's move away from its original set of interventions, which included making material donations to individual households. It replaced these material gifts with community education events, ECD centers, and support groups. I argue that although these changes were made in the name of increasing "community ownership" of the project, this public commitment ultimately prevented the staff from responding to the concerns that community members expressed. These concerns, I argue, were largely couched in terms of the ethics of the patron-client relationship described in chapter 2, and thus built around relationships of interdependence excluded by sustainable development.

In the second half, I show how participatory methods and a priori assumptions about the categories of people most in need ironically excluded the poorest children and families from programs run by Hope Child (and other NGOs in the area). I also demonstrate that quantitative data and photographs can obscure this shift from the most needy villagers to middle-class residents, the better to prove an NGO's work successful.

By exploring how the sustainable development assemblage shaped Hope Child's programs, I argue that development's failure to produce locally meaningful outcomes comes not from creating dependence but from attempting to avoid it. Some critics of development who promote the sustainable and participatory approaches I describe might argue, along with the Hope Child field staff, that villagers have become accustomed to sitting and waiting for handouts. I argue that while sustainable development may have thwarted some hopes for "handouts," the villagers still wait, giving their time and minimal resources to Hope Child in anticipation of some tangible benefit that the carefully crafted sustainable programming explicitly excludes. In the following pages I show that Hope Child did not fail to meet its written objectives; indeed, it generally reached its targets and produced measurable outputs. Yet despite its self-defined success and participatory aspirations, it failed by the standards defined by its beneficiaries.[3] I argue that Hope Child's locally defined failure was produced by its own commitment to community ownership.

Sebanda

Sebanda is forty kilometers outside the capital of Kampala, within the kingdom of Buganda. Most of the journey to Sebanda can be made on a paved two-lane highway, busy with white public minibus taxis,[4] private cars, and speeding lorries piled high with matooke[5] bananas or charcoal or loaded with cattle. Whizzing along crammed into one of these taxis, you pass identical-looking trading centers, with closely spaced houses, shops selling plastic basins and aluminum teakettles, and wooden stands piled high with cabbages, tomatoes, and avocados grown in family gardens or purchased wholesale from the central markets in Kampala.

The last ten kilometers into Sebanda, however, are down a badly rutted dirt road past single houses and small settlements, marked only by kiosks selling soap, sugar, and other household basics and by ubiquitous thatch-roofed bars selling fatty roasted pork and locally brewed beers and distilled spirits made from bananas, millet, or corn. On the final kilometer the taxi goes through a papyrus swamp, jutting in and out of puddles. At night you can hear frogs croaking and smell a stand of eucalyptus trees planted by a local agroforestry advocate. These sights and sounds mark the Sebanda subcounty.

When the taxi pulls into its final stop at the crossroads of a trading center, it is greeted by a large pack of young men on boda-boda[6] motorcycles, eager to ferry the taxi passengers to other locations in the subcounty. The trading center consists of bars selling bottled beer and sodas, small restaurants, and wholesale and retail kiosks hawking all manner of household goods. There is also a cluster of competing butchers who hack portions from quartered carcasses hanging from hooks on their wooden stalls. The butcher closest to the taxi stand has a wooden table piled with pink and white offal that he regularly washes down with water from a white plastic bucket.

Behind the official shops are small, densely packed brick buildings divided into one-room dwellings largely rented by single women caring for their children and grandchildren. Piles of garbage are burned in the late afternoon, filling the air with a haze from smoldering plastic bags. A marketplace built by the International Labor Organization in the early 1990s, as part of the reconstruction after the civil war that brought President Museveni to power, is now abandoned. It is possible to rent stalls in this marketplace from the subcounty government for a small fee, but no one does. There are also smaller shops and a warren of circular thatched huts filled with groups of men who can be found drinking at any hour.

The main roads are busy most of the day. Packs of children in bright pink and yellow uniforms are on their way home from Saint John's Primary School. Other children carry water from the boreholes[7] near the town center. Men push bicycles loaded with jerricans of water roped to the frames. The landless single women carry dirt-caked hoes and *pangas* (machetes), walking home from distant garden plots that they rent to grow their own food or dig for pay.

At night the trading center is loud. Several nights each month a commercial karaoke truck pulls into town loaded with six-foot-high speakers and a troupe of singers who perform the latest hits from the Ugandan pop music scene. On other nights there are all-night Christian concerts and prayer services organized by the local evangelical church. The church, not affiliated with Hope Child, obtains scholarships for some of its members' children through its connections with churches in the United States. The local Catholic Church runs a government-subsidized Universal Primary Education primary school and provides small scholarships, organized through Caritas International (an international Catholic NGO), for two hundred children regardless of their religious affiliation. These scholarships pay for school fees, lunches, and uniforms for students who could not otherwise afford to attend school. A nearby convent of Catholic nuns—who are primarily engaged in managing and staffing a large clinic in the trading center and who run a support group and medication-adherence program for HIV-positive women—also provides scholarships for secondary students in exchange for weekend work in the convent's gardens.

Away from the trading center, the roads are quiet. The villages blend one into the next with no real break between them. The houses vary: small rectangular houses made of sun-dried mud brick and with dirt floors stand next to more substantial stucco homes with glass windows and concrete floors. Nearly every house has a roof made of iron sheets; only the poorest people still use grass thatch. The houses have small gardens filled with rows of sweet potatoes, yams, and cassava, mango, papaya, and *matooke* banana trees, and coffee plants. Uganda remains a largely agrarian country, with more than 80 percent of the total workforce involved in small-scale subsistence farming and cash cropping. Unlike Kenya, where the British encouraged white farmers to establish large plantations, local farmers have historically raised most of the country's cash crops, including coffee and cotton, on small plots. This pattern continues, with many local subsistence farmers engaged in small-scale coffee production. Also found among the carefully cultivated plants are leafy green vegetables and towering jackfruit trees with their glossy green leaves and trunks bearing clusters of huge, spiny jackfruits.

During my fieldwork in Sebanda, I spent most of my time with Hope Child's two paid field staff members assigned to work in Sebanda: Martin Mugerwa and Sarah Nassali. Martin, who holds a bachelor of arts degree in social work, grew up in Kampala and is a member of the Baganda ethnic group. Having spent most of his life in the diverse middle-class milieu of the capital, he often said he felt more comfortable conversing in English than in his native Luganda. Martin rented a small room near the trading center in one of the few buildings with electricity. His permanent home is in Kampala, where his wife and children live. He also owns a small farm that he cultivates commercially using hired labor. Nassali, who also holds a bachelor of arts in social work, is a program officer; she was originally from Fort Portal in the west, and her parents are Congolese. She, her husband, and their children live in a rented house in the nearby market town.

I observed the daily activities of the Sebanda field office. I attended staff meetings at the field office and at the head office; observed community training and sensitization events; monitored visits from the head office; went on field visits to support groups, Early Childhood Development centers, and households; and sat in on meetings of community volunteers, a workshop organized by Hope Child's primary funder (the Netherlands-based Frans Lansing Foundation), and activities of ECD centers. In addition to these direct observations, I interviewed Hope Child staff members (7), Hope Child donors (4), Hope Child volunteers (10), Hope Child participants (9), members of the local government (10), and other local residents (18). I supplemented these in-depth interviews with a household survey that looked at socioeconomic status, NGO participation, political involvement, and residence patterns. I administered this survey to every household (140) within a single village where Hope Child was active.

Hope Child

Nancy Kabwende, a soft, slight, luminous woman from southwestern Uganda, built Hope Child out of an informal child helpline that she started in 1995. Although similar toll-free hotlines for seeking advice and reporting child abuse have long existed in more developed countries, Kabwende's was the first in Uganda.

When she began the child helpline, she was the national director of a large child-centered NGO and had previously worked as a district-level social welfare officer. In her autobiography, Kabwende writes, "In 1995 an inner voice said to me, 'You will be a comforter to hurting people.' I ignored it as just one of those thoughts. Two months later, I heard the same voice again, but this time it was louder than the first, 'You are going to be a savior of children.'" Responding to what she felt was a direct call from God, she listed her home telephone number in the newspaper, offering to listen to any hurting child who needed someone to talk to.

Over the next two months, she recruited two volunteers to help take calls and to rescue children in desperate circumstances. The organization grew with the support of numerous volunteers, many of them upper- and middle-class urban women who were financially supported by their husbands.

Hope Child's attention to the needs of the whole family set it apart from other orphan support organizations that worked more directly with the children. In focusing only on children, Hope Child argues, the other organizations failed to see the ongoing importance of widowed parents, grandparents, and other adults in the orphans' lives. Despite their visibility in popular media portrayals of AIDS orphans, child-headed households are only a tiny fraction of households caring for orphans in Uganda. To represent orphans as alone in the world not only devalues the important and difficult work done by their caregivers, but also provides an inaccurate image on which to base programming decisions. This makes it difficult to see the differences between the majority of orphans who are not alone and those few who truly have nowhere else to turn. In line with their efforts to support orphans and those who care for them, Hope Child's programs have now expanded to include a child abuse hotline; a microfinance scheme for caregivers; children's rights clubs; ECD centers for children under age eight; and the Grandparent Hope Network (GHN), which includes income-generating support groups both for grandparents caring for orphans and for ECD centers.

When Hope Child first began to pilot the GHN project in 2003, it set to work in a suburb of Kampala with a group of thirty households headed by grandparents. In addition to establishing community support groups and ECD centers, Hope Child gave these first thirty households mattresses, bedding, clothing, and sheets of iron for roofing. A mere four years later, however, such material assistance was rare, becoming so marginal to the organization's mission that the staff writing the GHN budget did not include material contributions at all. By the time Hope Child expanded its operations to the Sebanda subcounty in 2007, its strategy had shifted to align more closely with sustainable development, and such material gifts were now seen as unsustainable.

Instead, the GHN project was now centered on forming small groups, which were intended to provide social support and serve as bases for lending opportunities or projects to generate group income, such as raising poultry or pigs or growing produce to sell in local markets. Hope Child's work with these group undertakings was supplemented by frequent community meetings on such topics as malaria prevention, bookkeeping, child nutrition, and beekeeping. Community training on disease prevention, children's rights, and income-generating strategies was seen as more sustainable in that the knowledge could be passed on indefinitely.

Any material interventions that could be justified within sustainable development generally entailed durable structures that would outlast the program. At Hope Child, these durable structures were the Early Childhood Development centers. Over three years, Hope Child spent 43,700,000 UGX (US$25,700) building and furnishing the five centers and training volunteer caretakers to staff them. The ECD centers provide care, supervision, opportunities for play, and introduction to literacy and numeracy in English and Luganda, and five days each week they distribute cups of nutrisoy porridge to children under age eight, the cost subsidized by collecting tuition three times each school year.

In 2007–8, Hope Child was supported through grants from nearly a dozen private foundations and bilateral aid organizations like USAID, giving the GHN project an annual operating budget of more than US$375,000. The grants Hope Child receives come as gifts that need not be repaid. People outside the development industry imagine this money as flowing through NGOs like Hope Child to the people whose faces stare back from their glossy annual reports. Yet foundations like the Frans Lansing Foundation and NGOs like Hope Child, which operate using the tools of the sustainable development assemblage, must transform this money so that it is not simply transferred to the poor people they serve. These donations must be transformed into *programs* that can demonstrate a capacity for lasting change. Rather than being passed along to the poor as blankets, pigs, or school fees (as many in the rural subcounty of Sebanda imagined it would), the money is used for staff salaries, durable structures, community training sessions, vehicles to permit monitoring visits, research expenses, accounting consultants, seminars, and workshops. Within the ideal vision of sustainable development, one donation is enough, since if it is used properly it will engender an endless string of benefits. Sustainable development thus not only is posited as "the end of poverty"; it is also posited as the end of aid.

Despite Hope Child's growth and its success in securing funding from secular organizations in the United States and Europe, evangelical Christianity continues to be an important part of the organization's culture. Every morning members of the Kampala-based staff gather for an hour in the office's open-air atrium to sing and pray together. Staff members volunteer to read Bible passages aloud or offer testimonies about their faith experience. People pray about personal concerns during these daily sessions as well as the needs of the organization. Hope Child's ongoing commitment to Christianity, from its founding moment of Nancy Kabwende's divine calling and its early commitment to pragmatic gifts and empathetic listening through its recent embrace of secular models of sustainable development and its growing resistance to providing material and financial aid allows us to see how actors and organizations might draw on different ethical assemblages, either simultaneously or over time. The combination of religious practice and secular development strategies within the walls of Hope Child confirms Erica Bornstein's (2003) findings concerning the compatibility of Christianity and development. Yet, as I highlight in chapters 4 and 6 on Mercy House, not all Christian organizations have found this alliance so easy to broker, and many have continued to cling to more traditional forms of charity, despite the cost in terms of support from Western donors.

"You Can't Give Someone a Baby without Giving Them a Carrying Cloth"

Outspoken Hope Child beneficiaries often complained of the inadequacy of the material support provided. Beneficiaries and local volunteers alike protested that not only were the training sessions repetitive, but participants lacked the start-up capital to put the skills they learned into practice.

In discussing a recent agricultural training session in which people had been instructed in modern farming techniques but then given only seeds without any of the other inputs needed, Mary Nabukenya, a small-group leader, said of this minimal assistance: "You can't give someone a baby without giving them a carrying cloth." She was saying that it was point-less to give people a few seeds when Hope Child knew they would not also be given expensive fertilizer. On the other hand, Hope Child saw itself as encouraging self-reliance through gradual saving. In their eyes, villag-ers like Nabukenya should save up to buy fertilizer, a skill they would not learn if Hope Child simply handed it out. Yet in the eyes of Nabukenya and the other villagers, Hope Child was withholding its ample money and resources from loyal participants.

People throughout Uganda were critical of the seminars and training sessions offered by the various NGOs in the name of capacity building and sustainable development. The government of the Karamoja district, in the northeast of Uganda, banned all NGO seminars in April 2009, arguing that local leaders ought to be spending the critical period during the rainy sea-son readying their fields for planting, not attending meetings. The minis-ter for disaster preparedness was quoted in the national English-language newspaper *New Vision* as saying, "It is raining and you are wasting your time with workshops. . . . Use those billions you spend on baseline surveys and needs assessment studies to help the Karimojong have food security. Use that money to prepare gardens, dress Karimojong children and provide them with beddings" (Wanyama 2009).

Despite similar protests throughout Uganda, the seminars continued, at least in part because material assistance is poorly suited to the current cli-mate of international development work focused on cost-benefit analyses driven by a concern with quantifiable achievements, as I discuss further in chapter 5. It is far cheaper to help a large number of families or children when help is defined in terms of people attending a workshop rather than people assisted in more intensive ways.

This said, Hope Child constantly vacillates between its prior commit-ment to an ethics of charity and its new commitment to sustainable de-velopment. At the end of the last staff meeting of 2007, Nancy Kabwende stood before her staff members assembled under the tin roof of Hope Child's courtyard conference room. Kabwende, usually bright and smiling, looked exhausted, and she opened her remarks by telling about a recent conversation with God concerning Hope Child's plan to expand its ser-vices to reach ten thousand children: "I asked him how he expected me to take care of ten thousand children, and he told me I already was." Despite the changes in programming that limited the kinds of services Hope Child provided, Kabwende still saw "taking care" of all these children as a calling from God and felt she was being used as his instrument in the world. Yet she also doubted that her staff still saw their work as a calling, or a "form of ministry," and after saying she felt "like it was all over," she accused them of thinking of their work at Hope Child as "a job that can be done for money."

Throughout her speech, Kabwende shifted between images of "taking care" and telling stories of past instances of "child saving" and emphasizing the importance of avoiding "handouts." Despite real efforts to avoid handouts, success stories told at staff meetings and in Hope Child newsletters often hinged on providing them. Trying to inspire her staff, Kabwende recalled the case of two boys found living in the corner of a collapsed house. "We built them a house, found them a guardian, and paid for their schooling." This movement between actions based on policies and programs founded on sustainable community institutions and stories of idiosyncratic acts of charity was common at Hope Child staff meetings.

At a previous meeting, when asked to give some evidence of their success from the Kampala site, staff members reported that a longtime beneficiary, well known to the Hope Child staff, had been robbed. Hope Child decided to make her a gift of 500,000 UGX (US$294) from the "Nancy Kabwende Foundation," which enabled her to refurnish her home, pay her back rent, and start a restaurant. Ironically, stories like these were often used to demonstrate the success of Hope Child's programs, even though they ran counter to Hope Child's general position on handouts.

School Fees

The consequences of Hope Child's focus on making nonmaterial interventions and constructing permanent ECD centers can best be understood by contrasting these interventions with the local demand that Hope Child assist parents with their chief material challenge: school fees. The hardship of paying school fees is among the problems most frequently cited by parents and guardians in Uganda, as it is throughout much of the developing world, where quality schooling is not freely available. Despite the 1997 introduction of the Universal Primary Education (UPE) program in Uganda, in Sebanda families with children still needed to save large sums each year to pay for the tuition, uniforms, and exercise books needed to attend primary and secondary school. Based on a survey I conducted, an average family living in a village in Sebanda needed to save 150,000 UGX (US$88.23) each year to educate their children (the family with the highest annual fee burden was responsible for more than 2,500,000 UGX (US$1,471) in tuition and other fees). The amount families paid depended on how many children they had, how old the children were, and the school the parents selected. Given that most families in this area make their living primarily through subsistence farming and selling vegetables, livestock, and locally made bricks, saving this much cash is a monumental challenge.

Claims that school attendance was low because parents placed too little value on education were belied by people like Hasfah Nabasa, who lives with her four children in a windowless rented room with a dirt floor, behind the trading center. When I visited her home, the only light came from the doorway and through the holes in the roof. Nabasa had moved to Sebanda ten years earlier with her husband, who had been hired as an assistant to a local wholesaler. After moving to Sebanda, they had four children, who were now aged ten, five, four, and two. Her husband had left her one year before, so she was now totally responsible for the family's survival. Each morning she left to work in a rented garden, where she grew sweet potatoes and cassava. She also sold firewood and worked for pay in other people's gardens to raise the money to buy beans and groundnuts for food and to pay her children's school fees. Although there was a government-sponsored UPE school near her home, she had decided to send her children to Saint John's Primary School because she felt it offered a better education. "The standards of the UPE School are too low, and I'm afraid my children won't be able to compete [for jobs]." To send her three oldest children to Saint John's, she needed to save a total of 120,000 UGX (US$70.60) each year for their tuition and uniforms. Given her daily wage of 1,000 UGX (US$.60) and her need to pay rent and to buy food and other necessities like soap, salt, and kerosene for the lamp, she constantly struggled to keep her children in school. Her youngest child attended the Hope Child ECD center near her house and enjoyed it, "especially the porridge." With her enthusiasm for the ECD center, Nabasa hoped that Hope Child might eventually help her pay the primary school fees for her other three children.

Dorothy Namuli and Thomas Kigumba lived in a large concrete house; they were in considerably better financial shape than Nabasa, but they still struggled to pay school fees for the five children in their care, some of them orphaned relatives. Both were heavily involved as community volunteers; Dorothy not only volunteered as a zone leader for Hope Child but also served as the leader for women's affairs in the subcounty and had participated in programs run by seven other NGOs. Kigumba was serving as the elected village chairman and as a catechist in the Catholic Church, as well as working as an HIV/AIDS counselor and as a traditional healer. They had a considerably higher income than Nabasa from selling the milk from their cow, eggs from their chickens, and the fried snacks Dorothy made, besides income from the fees Kigumba charged for working as a healer. They also received transport allowances for their volunteer work. Even with these sources of income, they still strained to meet the costs of sending all five children to school. With several children in secondary school, their annual tuition burden was nearly 600,000 UGX (US$353).

Like Nabasa, Dorothy and Kigumba had originally hoped that Hope Child would help them in educating their children, either by paying the fees directly or by giving them capital to create projects that would significantly increase their income. During an interview Dorothy commented, "We were expecting a lot of help from them. Say, if you need a blanket, they give it to you; if it is a mattress, the same. . . . When they instituted the ECDs we thought that they would provide school fees for those above the ECD [age], but it wasn't possible. We still hoped that it could be done, but nothing; it seems that's where they wanted to end."

Hope Child staff members were well aware of this concern, since a baseline survey found that school fees were the most pressing problem for 95.3 percent of the village's families. Martha Sikolasi, the GHN program manager, agreed with the parents, "Whenever we have an evaluation, they keep saying school fees, school fees—and they're right. Where do you want them to go? Even the cheapest [school] would be 40,000 [UGX (US$23.52)]; if you're just selling charcoal [you can't afford it]."

Sarah Nassali was in agreement that school fees, especially secondary school fees, were the most pressing problem. One morning as we waited for the head office staff to arrive for a monitoring visit, she wondered out loud about the focus on the ECD centers. "Most families are able to manage with the young ones, but older children are more difficult. School fees are expensive, the real problem is poverty." Like Dorothy Namuli and Thomas Kigumba, Nassali argued that substantial income-generating activities (IGAs) should be at the center of any program meant to improve child and family well-being.

Yet despite Hope Child's general acknowledgment of poverty and the problems poor families face in paying school fees, program participants felt that Hope Child's primary intervention for addressing this problem—the children's rights clubs—failed to make any real impact. Hope Child's reliance on these clubs as a means of increasing school attendance is based on the assumption that parents' devaluation of education, not a lack of money, is the major barrier to children's school attendance. Hope Child used stories about the rare father who refused to send his child to school as proof that children's rights clubs were necessary. Yet most parents were very much in agreement that their children should attend school, so much so that Hasfah Nabasa was willing to tolerate gaping holes in her roof so her children could be educated in the same school as those more fortunate. The greater truth was that no matter how badly some parents wanted their children to attend school, their deep poverty meant they remained un-educated. But given the stringent demands of cost-effectiveness and project sustainability, directly financing these children's education was perceived as an impossible and irresponsible solution.[8]

Taking Ownership

The income-generating activities organized through the GHN support groups seemed to provide a more substantial answer. Many participants liked the IGA idea in theory, but as it was being implemented they com-plained that it could not work in reality. Dorothy Namuli told me, "They would help, but when [they] only give me 10,000 [UGX (US$5.88)], how do [they] expect me to make it valuable? It can only buy ropes for the ani-mals. It can't even buy a piglet. I accepted the money all right, but it can't change a lot. . . . So the person who is willing to help would donate some-thing bigger." Hope Child's commitment to the ethics of sustainable devel-opment and community ownership were the reasons it avoided donating "something bigger." Sarah Nassali argued that providing families or self-help groups with the cash needed to undertake substantial projects with-out requiring that they contribute money from their own savings would decrease their sense of "ownership," and that without it projects would likely fail.

During a round of routine visits to the GHN self-help groups, Nas-sali explained the importance of using something like a garden project to generate capital for a larger IGA in order to promote "project ownership" among the group members. If they were simply given the start-up capital, they would fail to value the project and might not put as much effort into it. As she told me, "If their pig dies, they should really feel it because it was something that was truly theirs and not something that had been given to them."

The ethical proposition that there was a need to create "project owner-ship" was echoed in my interviews with Elizabeth Makena, a Kenyan-born field officer with the Frans Lansing Foundation assigned to work with Hope

Child. She was as emphatic as Nassali that these families needed IGAs that could bring in enough money to pull their families out of the grinding poverty that kept children in danger of malnutrition and out of school. Yet she was as committed as Nassali to the ideals of community ownership that kept such IGAs from becoming a reality. In Makena's conceptualization, the GHN program was ultimately supposed to be the community's project, with Hope Child serving as a support, a "midwife." She was insistent that people ought to incorporate this thinking into the very language they used to discuss foundation-funded programs. She wanted people to talk about the projects not as belonging to the organization, but as belonging to the community. Community contributions thus became central to the work of Hope Child, and nothing was to be done without community involvement. Hope Child was there to help, but the real management and initiative were supposed to come from within the community. Yet, as I make clear in this chapter, it is implementation, not priority setting, that is ultimately ceded to the community.

In light of the commitment to community contributions, participants in Hope Child programs were regularly asked to contribute time and resources to running them. When visitors or funders were coming to see the project, participants gathered to slash the grass at the Hope Child field office compound and to cook for the guests. When ECD center buildings were being constructed, people were asked to contribute labor and bricks. Parents were expected to take turns providing the firewood and labor to cook the children's porridge every day. Each child attending an ECD center was required to pay 3,000 UGX (US$1.76) in tuition per term, with three terms each school year. Fees such as the ECD tuition are often talked about as community contributions, but they are in fact paid by individuals. Calling these fees community contributions masks their individual nature and the potential exclusion of those not able to pay.

Disappointments

Hope Child's demands for goods and collective labor closely mirrored the demands that chiefs, kings, and other patrons made on their clients and followers in Buganda. Ironically, what Hope Child saw as the community's taking ownership of the project, participants saw as a way of securing the support of a powerful patron and effectively entering into a dependency relationship.[9] For a time this misperception helped Hope Child achieve its goal of community participation. The enthusiastic response of participants like Miriam Namusaazi, who felt that being selected as cook for a major event might help her to secure a special "blessing," reflected this way of viewing the link between community participation and hopes for patron-client reciprocity. Most of the people I spoke with about their early experiences with Hope Child were like Namusaazi in looking forward to having Hope Child provide capital for their businesses, school fees for their children, and blankets for their beds. But after several months of voluntary service, they found that material gifts of bedding and school fees were not forthcoming.

As I noted above, many project beneficiaries viewed the refusal of material support with suspicion and privately accused the Hope Child staff and volunteers of "eating the money" intended for them. Those who made these accusations were implying that some staff members and volunteers were illicitly skimming money from the Hope Child budget, but I propose an alternative reading of the situation.

Despite the modesty of its field office, Hope Child's connections to wealthy foreign donors were obvious during the frequent donor site evaluations when Europeans and Americans arrived to inspect its work. These visits confirmed local belief that Hope Child had vast resources that the villagers knew were intended for their benefit. Yet by the time Hope Child paid its staff costs and the administrative overhead necessary for running the modest head office so as to comply with international standards for ensuring that the funds had been spent efficiently and effectively, there was little left to purchase things that the villagers could see and touch. Thus, after administering the new requirements for audit and accountability and meeting their commitment to economic sustainability, the Hope Child staff had no choice but to refuse the mantle of patronage that people so eagerly held out for them. And without material assistance for their work, the participants stopped volunteering. If Hope Child was not going to be the good patron, they were not going to waste their time being good clients.

The Vulnerable and the Worthy

Rescue Stage

Since its inception in 1995, Hope Child has defined children living in conditions of extreme vulnerability and poverty as its target population. Sarah Nassali explained that Hope Child tries to start working with families at the "rescue stage," hoping that over time they will move toward self-sufficiency. Village chairmen were accordingly instructed to identify the most vulnerable families in the community. Families defined as being at the "rescue stage" within Hope Child's model were those in crisis and unable to meet their basic needs. The force of the Frans Lansing Foundation and Hope Child's internal and external self-justification relied on an appeal to the suffering of the poorest and most helpless children. Elizabeth Makena emphasized the urgency of the foundation's work by saying, "For young children life is today and not tomorrow. If a three-month-old baby is hungry today she might be dead in another three months." Her colleague Peter Jansen also insisted that while their foundation was not interested in offering emergency financial relief, it did intend to work with the poorest people in any given community.

Given these statements, which we might understand as remnants from Hope Child's engagements with other ethical assemblages, we might expect that the poorest families in the village would fill Hope Child's case files. But this is not the case. While Hope Child's baseline survey found that 31.4 percent of potential beneficiaries could afford only one meal a day and graphically described the damaging effects of malnutrition, many of these families were not chosen for inclusion in the program. Analysis of my own household-level survey data on socioeconomic status and NGO participation revealed that only one of the thirteen families sending their children to a village-level Hope Child crèche (7 percent) ate only one meal a day. The remaining twelve ate two or more meals a day, even though six other eligible families in Hope Child's catchment area who reported eating only one meal a day did not send their children to the crèche. Given the goal of reaching families at the "rescue stage," one would expect a higher percentage of extremely poor families in the program.

I also found that eligible people at the middle third of the local socioeconomic ladder were three times as likely to participate in Hope Child's programs as those at the bottom third.[10] These quantitative data were confirmed by Waswa Charles, Sebanda's government-appointed community development officer: "If someone came targeting the most vulnerable, they are not the families being assisted. That is the problem. . . . One time I was walking [and] found an old man seated with a hoe, cultivating. You can imagine! . . . Maybe he doesn't associate with those who select. Such persons are neglected."

Charles's comments not only support my observations concerning the exclusion of the poorest members of the community; they also highlight the role of obligations to kinsmen, friends, political supporters, and other clients in determining who will benefit from local development projects. There is little doubt that these dynamics were in play when local leaders and experienced NGO volunteers were asked to help determine who would be interviewed during the baseline survey and who was ultimately placed on the roster of beneficiaries.

Thus the sustainable development assemblage, local alliances, and judgments that the village elite make about the poor have shifted the program's target population and focus, and this shift has partially been obscured by qualitative and quantitative reporting techniques that both make and erase distinctions between segments of the rural population. These erasures eased residual ambivalence about the mission of the organization.

Resourceful People

In addition to the role personal connections played in determining who would be considered for NGO participation, there were local ideas akin to Euro-American notions of the "worthy poor," defined locally as those who could best take advantage of what the program offered. Nalongo Kasule, a woman volunteering with multiple NGOs, argued that families who were not willing or able to participate fully should be left out of NGO programming. This view was common among community leaders, who argued that NGOs should focus on the hardworking people who were most likely to take advantage of all their interventions.

Namiro Ruth is one such industrious woman whom many NGOs were happy to include as a participant. At the back of her compound she had a large, well-constructed pen holding two adult pigs and seven piglets, two of which belong to the support group she leads. The pen, with its concrete floor, wooden walls, and well-made reed roof, made me think this was perhaps the work of a very dedicated GHN support group, and I wondered if they had received additional help from Hope Child. As it turned out, the piggery was in existence before Hope Child came to Sebanda and was Namiro's private initiative. The GHN support group had saved enough money to buy two piglets and supplied their feed, but otherwise this was her own project.

Nevertheless Nassali exclaimed, "They just went to the training and came home and did this!" assuming that the piggery was the result of the GHN support group's efforts. George, my assistant, asked Namiro how she had raised the capital to start the piggery. She said she had sold her cow. She had been to a workshop where the vice president of Uganda promised piglets to anyone who could build them a pen. She sold her cow, bought the materials, and started building. The promised piglets never appeared, but she was able to buy a few with money left over from selling the cow. It was not only her initiative, but also her access to capital that enabled her to start the piggery.

This scene was repeated at the home of Matthew Mulindwa, a Hope Child volunteer and support group chair in the trading center. At the back of his house a large chicken coop was being constructed out of bricks, with separate floors for roosters, hens, and chicks. The building had come to a temporary stop because the wife of the builder Mulindwa had hired was sick. Mulindwa said he planned to donate the chicken coop to the group, but that if the group disintegrated it would come back to him. Nassali was impressed by this and by the smaller wooden chicken coop she saw as the seed of this larger project. "Look at his ability to take advantage of the training; if only everyone had his initiative." Nassali continued, "There are some people here who really know about farming." Nassali's exuberant celebration of Mulindwa's chicken coops reflects her judgment of his ethical worthiness as someone who works hard and takes advantage of situations. He is seen not as having resources, but as resourceful. She seemed not to consider other sources of wealth coming in. I became aware of these when George pulled me aside and suggested that the capital for the larger project had likely come from Mulindwa's son, who lives and works abroad. He pointed out the television antenna on top of the house and the electric wires connecting the home to the intermittent electricity supply. Nassali's slippage between people with resources and resourceful people is not without some logic. People who work hard and save are likely to have more resources in the future. But thinking about Mulindwa's resourcefulness in this way ignores the advantages his family may have. Nassali argued that other people had not really taken advantage of all the opportunities presented to them. But seizing opportunities takes time and money that for some families could mean the difference between eating and not eating.

Rosemary Nakato, a skilled participant in numerous NGOs, said she and others in the area were troubled by high microfinance interest rates and demands for community contributions. They wondered why the NGOs insisted on operating this way. She said to me, "We wonder sometimes, 'You find me with nothing, you say you want to help me, but you are saying I have to invest first. Now, where do I get the money from? If you are to help me, do it unconditionally.' And when they see someone who has [money], then they give him more money. Because that person can build a structure of cement." In thinking about the requirements of participation and community contributions, we find an answer to Rosemary's questions. Using existing resources to determine someone's worth is highly compatible with the technologies of sustainable development. As I noted above, sustainable development requires people to actively engage with development efforts by taking part in groups, coming to meetings and education sessions, and making regular contributions of time, money, and other goods. The poorest people in Sebanda had neither the time nor the money to make these contributions and efforts. They either were too busy trying to survive or lacked the wherewithal to participate in a way acceptable to Hope Child. The adolescent members of the children's rights clubs told me that the children in greatest danger of contracting HIV and dropping out of school were those whose parents were not hardworking or who spent all the family's resources drinking at the bars in the trading center. These children were not part of the clubs, nor were their parents members of Hope Child. They were not considered the "worthy poor" by the local leaders and were thus not considered for NGO participation. These parents were unlikely to make the contributions of time and money that Hope Child and other NGOs required as demonstrations of active participation. Fear of being asked to sign their names also made illiterate people reluctant to come to meetings held by NGOs. It is not surprising that those in Hope Child's programs were often already active in numerous other local NGOs, community-based organizations, and government programs, which all made similar demands on their participants.

Community Contributions

This situation was reinforced by the knowledge that the GHN support groups stressed savings, either by individuals or as a group. Each participant was to contribute a small amount of money at every meeting, to be saved toward a large purchase. Many rural families were able to spare a few hundred shillings each week, but for others even such a small amount entailed a major sacrifice, such as not buying salt for cooking. Families who knew they could not make the regular contributions either declined to join a GHN support group or were not asked.

Urban Ugandans, who participate in an economy distinct from that of poor rural farmers, have trouble understanding the significance of such small sums, and this understanding is harder for employees of international foundations. Even within the village, the significance of small amounts of money varied from family to family. The 3,000 UGX (US$1.76) ECD center contribution might be small for some people yet prohibitive for others. User fees or the need to make material contributions to projects likely helped explain why people told me they did not have the money to take part in programs of the numerous NGOs operating in the subcounty. And there were certainly some who would rather use their limited resources for other purchases. As I noted above, children whose parents could not put their education first were likely most at risk and thus most in need of the programs Hope Child sponsored. Yet given the required community contribution, such children were excluded.

Contributions need not refer only to money or material goods. People's time and effort in planning and carrying out a project are just as central to the concept of ownership. Within the logic of Hope Child and the Frans Lansing Foundation, community participation was essential to "taking ownership" of a project.

In early November 2007, I accompanied the Hope Child field staff when they visited each of the support groups to assess and encourage such community participation. Alongside the children's rights clubs and ECD centers, the support groups are intended to raise the incomes and the spirits of the adults heading participating families.

After a brief stop at the ECD center, we walked to the first of the support groups with Dorothy Namuli. She brought us over to a group of three women working with *pangas* and hoes to dig postholes for a piggery. The group had managed to save enough for one piglet. The group member who owns the land where the pigpen was to be placed had some other pigs. Their digging could not have been better timed. Nassali was visibly pleased that they were all working together. The timing seemed so good that I wondered if the work had been planned to coincide with the monitoring visit. All the holes were newly dug, and given that the group had been formed the previous May and our visit took place in November, it seemed unlikely that they just happened to begin work on the day of the visit.

Another support group also made sure their efforts were timely, though at least some members did seem to find value in the project itself. We cheered their well-tended bed of eggplants and green peppers. Yet when I asked Nassali how much she hoped the produce would bring, she estimated 10,000 UGX (US$5.88). Nassali realized that this was not much when split among eight people, yet she argued that collective work was good in itself and that people should take part in the IGA to better themselves. If they did not, she said, it was probably because they were lazy and not committed to the group enterprise. Given the ethical value the sustainable development assemblage placed on collective work, nonparticipants were morally suspect.

The positive valuation of collective work is one of the more interest-ing normative aspects of sustainable development, given the simultaneous commitment to neoliberal ideals of self-help and entrepreneurship. The dual commitment to neoliberalism and something verging on socialism reveals the dividing line between the community—idealized as an altruis-tic and egalitarian collective—and the outside world, which is considered separate and with no moral obligation to participate in that collective. The collective also becomes a monitoring body that will ensure that microloans are repaid. The multifunctional nature of the collective—serving the pur-poses of debt collection, social support, and mutual aid and acting as so-cialist enterprise, state substitute, and long-term panacea for the end of aid—makes it highly attractive to potential donors and aid workers across the political spectrum.

Several groups seemed to have put little effort into their projects, pre-senting a problem given the moral imperative to work as a group. At the home of one group leader, there was a sad little plot with cabbages and rad-ishes planted haphazardly and left unweeded. The garden was a depressing contrast to the woman's own well-tended *matooke* plantings. George com-mented that it reminded him of his childhood. "When I was about four or five, my mother gave me a small plot about that size so I could learn to farm. I would plant the little cabbages and tend the plot, then we would all enjoy eating the produce for supper," he said. He was proud of his child-hood garden but found it laughable that this untended plot was the work of eight adults. "Perhaps these people do not see this as important work; perhaps they are just making a minimal effort to please the project staff." He added, though, "Even with a good yield a plot like this couldn't [fetch] more than about 2,000 UGX [US$1.18]." This poorly tended garden was taken as a sign of the group's failure. That the members had simply decided the project was not worth their time and chose to tend their own gardens was not conceivable.

Self-Sufficient Strangers

These demands for community contributions of material resources and labor not only recall the demands made by patrons, but also create a situ-ation where the ideal NGO participant is extremely poor yet still able to contribute to the project. Yet the poorest people often lack the necessary cultural capital, resources, and time. Many of the poorest people in Sebanda also drank heavily or had a disability and so were generally excluded. Hope Child and other NGOs substituted people who seemed more likely to take advantage of the opportunities presented. While certainly poor compared with people in wealthy countries like the United States or even with the Hope Child staff, these substitutes actually were on the middle rungs of the village socioeconomic ladder and did not face the extreme poverty their neighbors endured. Although focusing on the middle class is not questionable in itself, that this de facto focus was not reflected in the program's design did create several problems. High-risk populations explicitly targeted, such as children not attending school, were not reached, lessening the impact of Hope Child's AIDS prevention programs. In addition, the forms of material support available through Hope Child were generally small. Although a mosquito net or a very small injection of capital might make some difference in the life of a very poor person, Dorothy Namuli's earlier comment reveals how little difference such a contribution makes to someone in the middle of the local socioeconomic hierarchy. If someone is too poor to buy a piglet or a rope for their animals, 10,000 UGX (US$5.88) will make some difference, but if someone needs to buy a cow or enough concrete to build a piggery to significantly improve their family's economic well-being, 10,000 UGX is unlikely to make much difference.

The de facto refusal to engage the poorest of the poor is theoretically resolved by an appeal to the ideals of African community. Elizabeth Makena first articulated this during our conversation in 2007 when she emphasized the urgent need to help young children in danger of dying from starvation. As we sat in leather armchairs in the lobby of a luxury hotel in Kampala where the Frans Lansing Foundation was sponsoring a conference for its East African partners, she explained, "We're looking to strengthen the community and the family safety net. This will eventually serve to help everyone in the end. . . . The most vulnerable don't have time for meetings, but by strengthening community cohesion you will be able to help them indirectly." Makena's plan relies on this community cohesion. The poorest of the poor will eventually benefit from the community safety net. Her theory of the safety net ironically reflects something akin to trickle-down economics and what I think of as the ideal-typical African village. This imaginary village is built on the assumption that people have a natural regard for the well-being of their fellows. Yet the most vulnerable in Sebanda often fell outside this proposed safety net, which generally follows lines of kinship rather than geography. Those at greatest risk of lacking food, education, and basic medical care were the children of recent immigrants to the area or of parents who drank heavily or had been rejected by their extended families. Indeed, the judgments made by local people who were in a position to assist their poor neighbors and kin through ethics of patronage mirrored those made by NGO workers advocating for sustainable development. It has long been true in Buganda that people who show promise are more likely to be taken on as clients. Thus in this instance we find congruence rather than conflict between indigenous ethics of patronage and sustainable development.

The subtle but profound local economic differences between the poorest of the poor and people who ultimately participate in NGO programs like those run by Hope Child are in large part ignored by the international funders living in countries like the Netherlands or the United States, as well as those in Uganda's cities. These differences are obscured through statistics and images that describe a population in abject poverty. Percentages and numerical tables are used to assure the readers, and perhaps the writers, of Hope Child's reports that the poorest people have been identified, and that the choice of projects will influence the selection of participants.[11] It is not so much that Hope Child's survey methods fail to count the poorest people as that their exclusion from the program has been hidden by the publication of counts that included them.

For example, until recently the poorest people in the community were the focus of program reports, and they were also highly visible in most of Hope Child's electronic and print publications despite their falling presence in its programs. People were photographed in front of mud houses, the main stories described only the most desperate cases, and the words "needy" and "vulnerable" were frequently deployed. Statistics, stories, and photographs pictured program beneficiaries as extremely old and poor. But looking more closely at the data on the actual participants and comparing them with their nonparticipating neighbors reveals that, in reality, resourceful middle-class people have in many cases been chosen to participate and have in a way been substituted for the people who fit the statistical and photographic images, as noted above. This switch is hidden by publishing photos that seem to prove that Hope Child participants are extremely poor, and by statistics showing the presence of extreme poverty in the area. The unpleasant task of deciding between working with those most in need or with those who will participate most actively is thus avoided and left unspoken.

There are signs, however, of a subtle shift now taking place in Hope Child's representational strategies. The importance of sustainable development and its effects on the target population are being registered by a shift in the photographic rhetoric of its more recent publications. In September 2008 Hope Child's website underwent a transformation, with happier, more self-sufficient children and grandparents replacing the hollow eyes and swollen bellies of its earlier visuals. Not only were the photos themselves better composed and in higher resolution; they represented a critical shift in the organization's public image.

This shift aligns closely with movements in the contemporary culture of development, which prizes self-sufficiency and community ownership. The Frans Lansing Foundation has been explicit about its decision to use pictures of happy, hopeful children and caregivers. The website states: "[We] always [try] to use images that give issues a human face, that show optimism in the face of difficulty, and that show potential and capacity." Mary Andersen, the foundation's head of publications, writes, "While most photo agencies have numerous images that depict children in disadvantaged circumstances, they usually portray children as victims, often in dismal surroundings, and without any apparent hope or prospect. We believe this has a numbing effect and enhances the flawed image that most people have of developing countries and of poverty in general."

In this movement we see the "suffering stranger" described by Leslie Butt (2002) in her critique of images and stories of named but voiceless suffering others being replaced by the "self-sufficient stranger." In part we can see this movement as a shift from a humanitarianism focused on alleviating physical and psychological suffering in the present to a model of development oriented toward economic growth and future well-being (Bornstein and Redfield 2011). This new developmental star is ready to transform the world with only an opportunity, a workshop, or a microfinance loan. Whereas the informal economy was previously seen as a symptom of poverty, it has come to represent an opportunity to be exploited by the microentrepreneurs who are now held up as the newest panacea for ending poverty (Elyachar 2005).

Although the "suffering stranger" exaggerated the impotence of the world's poor, this new happy image carries its own danger. This new model of participatory practice visually rendered through smiling faces further erases the needs and voices of the poorest of the poor from the global vision. Their faces have been replaced with those of their more prosperous neighbors, who seem like better candidates for sustainable development. We should not be lulled into thinking the people themselves have been transformed; it is only that the focus of the cameras and the programs has shifted.

Conclusion

In this chapter I have described the sustainable development assemblage and outlined several of the problems that arose during its use at Hope Child. I have argued that its commitment to nonmaterial interventions and community ownership prevented Hope Child from developing programs that would meaningfully address community priorities. As the ideologies and technologies, norms and practices of sustainable development strengthen their influence over the interventions designed by a range of actors, we must attend to the particular forms of ideological deafness that this assemblage has produced. Development workers afflicted by this deafness may no longer hear requests for material assistance. Requests for school fees, sheet-iron roofs, and farm implements are not allowed to be the answer, so the quest continues for more acceptable solutions to the question, What do you need?

Hope Child's refusal to distribute material resources and its attempts to promote community ownership through collective labor and community contributions ultimately produced a situation where many previously enthusiastic volunteers privately accused Hope Child of corruption and stopped volunteering. Hope Child accused these same people of being lazy and uninterested in their own development. By the time I returned to Sebanda in 2010, there was little left of the GHN project. Whereas Hope Child and the residents of Sebanda subcounty blamed each other for the project's failure, I argue that many of the problems encountered were unavoidable given the techniques, values, and ways of thinking rooted in the sustainable development assemblage. And despite participants' claims that Hope Child had failed, I argue that it succeeded, at least on its own terms. Based on the number of ECD centers built, banana-fiber dolls made, ECD caretakers trained, workshops held, stakeholder meetings convened, reports written, and GHN support groups organized, it was incredibly successful, and this success has been rewarded by the many donors who continue to rank it at the top of their funding portfolios.

FOUR

"Love Is the Answer": Charity and Kiganda Ethics of Interdependence

When I arrived in Uganda in 2007, I wanted to study NGOs working with orphans and vulnerable children, though not particularly orphanages or children's homes. These locations seemed marginal to the models being used by most local and international NGOs active in Uganda. Nevertheless, in deference to my host father, Evarist Musumba, a retired civil servant who was eager to introduce me to the people he knew who were working with orphans, I had agreed to visit several of these homes, all run by small communities of African nuns.

Mercy House, in Namayumba, was one of them, and one morning in late June 2007 I made my way through the chaos of the taxi park and got into the run-down public taxi that would take me there. After lurching down many miles of muddy roads, we arrived at the wide crossroads of the Namayumba trading center. On getting out of the taxi, I met a young man, Engoa John, riding a hand-propelled three-wheeled wheelchair. He introduced himself with a smile and asked where I was going. He said he worked as a vocational training instructor at Mercy House and offered to show me the way.

Leaving behind the bustle of shops and *boda-boda* motorcycles, we passed a large hospital complex and a stately brick chapel surrounded by a carefully tended garden of dahlias, roses, and citrus trees. As we went past Mercy House's primary- and secondary-level Catholic schools and the housing for the Franciscan Sisters of Africa and the novices, John told me about his work teaching shoemaking in Mercy House's vocational training program. Turning a corner, we came to an open iron gate leading into the central courtyard of Mercy House. The compound was quiet, since most of the children were in school. A few teenagers from the vocational training program were sitting on the concrete steps of a burned-out building, chatting as they watched people come and go.

When we arrived at the sisters' cottage, the cook told us that Sister Valentine Ngendo, Mercy House's second-in-command, was working in the garden, and John said I should wait for her in the sisters' sitting room. As I waited alone on the doily-covered turquoise sofa, I took note of the homemade papier-mâché bust of a white nun, perched on the shelf, wearing an old-fashioned wimple and wire-rimmed glasses.

After some time Sister Valentine came in to show me around the compound. Her youth and energy surprised me, since in the United States, where I grew up, most nuns I had encountered were nearing or well past retirement age. As I struggled to keep up with her long strides, she told me about Mercy House and its charges, including children, adolescents, and the elderly. I was impressed with the range of projects Mercy House was involved in and moved by the extreme circumstances the residents had come from. Yet I felt that its charitable works were marginal to the larger story of NGO-based development that I wanted to tell, and I confirmed that I did not want to pursue Mercy House as a field site.

But after four months of fieldwork with Hope Child in Sebanda, the significance of Mercy House, and of charity work more generally, began to come clear. I came to see Mercy House's offerings of unsustainable charity as an important counterpoint to the sustainable development projects I was studying, because it is against exactly this sort of charity that sustainable development advocates frame their work. With my opinion changed, in November 2007 I made a weeklong visit to Mercy House to explore working there as a second field site. After I explained the details of my study, the sisters and the residents agreed to my writing about the work of Mercy House, and in early December my husband, Paul, and I moved from Sebanda to Kampala. From Kampala, I was able to travel regularly to Namayumba, generally staying for a week at a time in the order's guesthouse while continuing to make trips to Sebanda to follow the work of Hope Child. At Mercy House I spent my days observing activities and talking with the sisters, the residents, and the steady stream of volunteers who came to donate their time through an array of self-defined projects.

I spent my evenings in the sisters' house, talking with them in their sitting room or over home-cooked dinners of *matooke*, rice, and fish soup and jugs of passion fruit juice. Once we were all exhausted from talking, they would escort me across the road to the guesthouse. The cool night air, dense with the buzzing of mosquitoes near the lake, was often filled with the practicing of Mercy House's brass band, including a massive sousaphone donated by a German monk. Much of what I learned at and about Mercy House felt like the inexplicable and uncalculated presence of that sousaphone.

In this chapter I describe how my fieldwork at Mercy House revealed the contours of an ethical assemblage that has coalesced from the interplay between Kiganda ethics and the vestiges of older forms of Catholic charity, which predate, and differ from, contemporary Catholic social teaching. In the daily actions of the sisters at Mercy House, one can see evidence of the reciprocal obligations of secular patronage networks and of the less reciprocal exchanges motivated by *omutima omuyambi*, what was described to me as the inborn "heart for helping." For more than a century, these two Kiganda ethics—secular patronage and *omutima omuyambi*—have played out in relation to the ethics of Catholic charity in Uganda. It is in this space that the Franciscan Sisters of Africa and other Ugandan Christians have created a new ethical assemblage with elements of both. Unlike Hope Child, which applies the logic of sustainable development in considering how to help the poor, no matter what their actual needs might be, Mercy House follows other rules. At Mercy House the sisters, residents, and some volunteers follow an ethics of unsustainable charity. This does not mean there were no disagreements between the sisters and the residents, but rather that conflicts and complaints were voiced in a shared language of the good.

My aim here is not only to show this assemblage as a way of speaking to the dynamics of hybridity and globalization (Tsing 2005) but, more important, to speak to the ways the productivity of both charity and patronage is resisted by scholars and members of the international development community (Douglas 1990; Farmer 2003; Stirrat and Henkel 1997) because of their discomfort with dependence, inequality, and the coexistence of care and power. This chapter serves as the crux of my examination of Western assumptions about the negative effects of dependence. I argue that these presuppositions lead many to disregard the ways being a dependent is valued in Uganda as a key path for social mobility, to ignore the agency involved in seeking out a patron, and to neglect the fact that clients are also frequently the patrons of others.

As I wrote in chapter 1, denunciations of charity and patronage not only are topics in the literature on development but also are central to anthropological writings on exchange. In closing this chapter I will reflect on these denunciations by exploring the literature on gift-debt relationships and charity, ultimately laying out a critique of Bourdieu's (1977) work on charity as a form of symbolic violence. By attending to how certain forms of hierarchical care can create solidarity rather than difference, and by conceptualizing charitable gifts as changing both givers' and receivers' expectations of reciprocity, I aim to represent experiences of charity in Uganda using a more nuanced reading of these actors' understandings and the complex interactions between them.

Mercy House

Mercy House is one of the more than thirty convents established by Mother Mary Patrick in Uganda, Kenya, and Tanzania. Mother Mary Patrick came to Uganda from Ireland in 1906 as a Franciscan missionary, and in 1923 she founded an order of African sisters, the Franciscan Sisters of Africa. Mother Mary Patrick originally established Mercy House on the grounds of the order's hospital in Kampala, which she opened in 1908. She conceived of Mercy House as a place where people with debilitating diseases could live and receive care after their discharge from the hospital. Over time, Mercy House also became a home for both the very young and the very old who had no one else to care for them.

In 1928 Mercy House was moved to a site across the road from the newly established motherhouse in Namayumba, so that "the sisters who had professed could bring food to the poor." Mercy House was moved not so much so that the poor might have food as to let the newly professed sisters practice the form of charity that they saw as at the center of their Franciscan charism.[1] Charity was not only the means of helping the poor but an end in itself. It was conceived as a way sisters could enact their love and devotion to God and neighbor in a highly intentional effort to form themselves and each other as particular kinds of Christian subjects. (I will return to this point in more detail in chapter 6.)

The Franciscan Sisters of Africa

Six sisters carried out most of the day-to-day work of managing Mercy House in 2007–8, though none had come there by choice. Although they had all joined the order of their own volition, a committee of superiors assigned them to specific locations, moving them from post to post with surprising frequency. The superiors explained these moves as necessary to the functioning of the order, which was stretched thin across its many projects, and as keeping the sisters from becoming too attached to any one project.

These six sisters' most immediate supervisors were Sister Grace Jata and Sister Kathleen Namuli, who oversaw the order's work in the central region. These two sisters were supervised in turn by Mother Perpetua Kadama, who was at that time the mother superior for the entire order of nearly 250 sisters who worked at sixty-four mission convents, running schools, hospitals, and other programs throughout Uganda, Kenya, and Tanzania. Several of the order's sisters also reported directly to funders, mostly small European or American foundations. For reasons of religion or because they saw them as trustworthy, these funders were particularly interested in working with women religious. The salaries these organizations paid the sisters were not theirs to keep but were turned over to the order for the upkeep and ministries of all their sisters.

The head of the home during the first half of my fieldwork was Sister Caroline Kagoya. She had been raised in a village in eastern Uganda[2] and had been at Mercy House since 1998. In addition to her duties there, she worked with similar homes run by the Franciscan Sisters of Africa in eastern and northern Uganda and with the Junior Franciscans (JUNFRA), a youth club designed to support teenagers, mostly Catholic, and mold them into good Christians. In the evenings, Sister Caroline would often lean back in her chair, her heavy body exhausted from visiting these distant projects, while she spoke enthusiastically about planting wheat for the bakery in eastern Uganda or extending JUNFRA to northern Uganda, with a sense that God would provide for these projects as he saw fit. The other sisters and volunteers privately worried that Sister Caroline's plans seemed more expansive than even Providence would allow.

Sister Valentine, the first sister I met when I originally visited Mercy House, was from Kenya and had worked as a director of secular development projects before joining the order. When I met her in 2007, she had worked at Mercy House for more than a decade and knew a lot about the home's recent history. Given Sister Valentine's sharp mind and strong organizational skills, many funders were eager to see her rise in the order's hierarchy and vied to have her assigned to their special projects. Camilla Korteweg, founder of the Netherlands-based Bread for the World, had won this competition for the time being, and Sister Valentine had been assigned to run a Bread for the World bakery at Mercy House, as well as to oversee the expansion of the Bread for the World project at several other Franciscan Sisters of Africa missions in Uganda.

Sister Sylvia Birungi—a tiny, bookish woman from Buganda, in her early thirties—was by far the most reserved of the sisters and was one of several professed nuns and priests in her family. Peering through her round glasses above a mug with a letter S printed in delicate scrollwork, she regularly offered her commentary on the happenings at Mercy House while generally keeping her distance from the chaos. Sister Sylvia was deeply committed to her daily prayers and always managed to break away from her work to attend the evening liturgy of the hours. She had recently made her final profession and liked to show off the silver ring that marked her new commitment. She primarily helped manage the bakery, but she also taught classes in cooking and nutrition in Mercy House's vocational training program.

During the first half of my fieldwork, Sister Jane Nabaggala served as the primary social worker for the home, overseeing the welfare of the nearly 150 people living there. Sister Jane was born in 1977 in a village in Buganda near Lake Victoria. Her parents had divorced when she was very young, and over time I learned that her story was not unlike those of many of the orphaned and abused children who arrived at Mercy House's gate seeking care and shelter. After her parents divorced, she went to live with her father and stepmother, but she did not stay long. "My stepmother beat us," she explained, "and so we left and went to stay with my grandma." Her grandmother was poor and had trouble feeding the children, so Jane and her brothers suffered from kwashiorkor[3] and other illnesses: "We used to tease each other, pointing at each other's swollen bellies and joking about who was going to die first." When she was thirteen she left her grandmother and moved in with her uncle, who gave her the job of taking care of his many pigs. He said she could go to school. "I had never been to school," she said, "but at thirteen it would be too humiliating to enter primary one, so I said I would go if I could start at primary four." Her uncle agreed, and when she went to the deputy headmaster of the school, four miles from her uncle's home, she told him she had studied up to primary three but had hidden in the bush during the war, disrupting her schooling. She told me, "I showed him some scars on my legs and told him I had gotten them in the bush during the war running in the sharp grass and pointed sticks." The headmaster believed her story and agreed to let her start in primary four. "I struggled, since I didn't know how to write and didn't speak any English. I didn't even know how to hold a pen and could fill a whole page [writing] one letter M." Luckily she made friends who helped her study in the afternoons, and in the evenings her uncle helped her prepare for the next day's lessons. That first year she was five places from the bottom of the class, but by the time she took her primary leaving exam three years later, she was among the top five. Tragically, her uncle died the next year, leaving her with one pregnant pig as her inheritance. "That pig gave birth, and I was able sell off the piglets, always keeping one or two . . . and so gradually increased my piggery." Using the money from selling the pigs, she was able to pay her own school fees through secondary four, and she even paid the school fees for several other poor children in the village. "Even now when

I go back, they expect me to be rich since I always had money back then from what I was making raising my pigs." Sister Jane eventually found her calling through her friendship with Sister Christine Namusoke, an elderly member of the Franciscan Sisters of Africa who still worked as a catechist in the lakeside communities near Namayumba, where Sister Jane's uncle had lived. The parallels between Sister Jane's own experiences and those of the residents of Mercy House not only shaped how she interacted with the children, but also showed the ways a person might be a giver or a receiver at different moments in life.

In 2008 Sister Jane, then thirty-one, was asked to serve as the mother superior of Mercy House, even though she was still a year away from making her final profession. Although she was visibly nervous about assuming such a great responsibility, she agreed and was taking over the leadership of the home when I left in April 2008. Many of the sisters were glad to see her step into this role and felt the home might be more organized under her leadership than under Sister Caroline's. Given her close involvement with the residents, the other sisters saw her as singularly dedicated to the work of Mercy House and to the welfare of the people living there. And so, despite her youth and lack of experience, they welcomed her tenure as mother superior.

During 2007–8, the sisters were assisted by thirteen paid staff members. Many of them had no special training and were hired at minimal salaries to serve as matrons (four), watchman (one), agricultural workers (four), community outreach workers (two), and cooks (two). Owing to a chronic shortage of funds, these workers complained that they were often paid late, leading to frequent staff turnover. Others, including an occupational therapist who was privately funded by a German-based NGO in Kampala and John, the shoemaking instructor in the vocational training school, were more highly skilled and thus better paid. Several European and American volunteers were also deeply involved in the life of Mercy House during my fieldwork, including Monica Richards, a Peace Corps volunteer who was working on Mercy House's community rehabilitation efforts, and Ruth Petersen, a second Peace Corps volunteer who arrived in spring 2008.

Nearly everyone working at Mercy House agreed that the home was badly understaffed, both by sisters and by paid employees. When an older nun, Sister Deborah Nankisa, was moved from her longtime post at Mercy House to work with the retired sisters living in the Saint Balikuddembe convent in Namayumba, she was never replaced. Neither was a replacement sent for Sister Caroline, who was reassigned in spring 2008. Even with these transfers, Sister Jane had trouble persuading their superiors to assign more sisters to Mercy House. Despite its significance in the history of the order and the crucial role it has played in the sisters' charism, the order was aided financially by the salaries the nuns brought in by working in the more lucrative boarding schools and hospitals, which funded the order's administration, the training of new sisters, and care for the elderly nuns in their retirement community. Tensions between ensuring the sustainability of the order and living out a life centered on voluntary poverty and charitable giving were central to the arguments within the order.[4]

In light of these staffing problems, when Sister Jane took over as the mother superior, she became responsible for running the home while continuing to serve as the social worker for all the children and other residents. When Ruth, Mercy House's second Peace Corps volunteer, arrived to take up her post, she asked Sister Jane if they could get more matrons to act as mothers to small groups of children. Sister Jane's eyes filled with tears and she told Ruth, "That sounds wonderful, but that would cost almost 5 million UGX (US$3,000), and the chance of having the money to do something like that is almost impossible. And if at some point in the future we weren't able to get the money, we would be left with people we couldn't pay." Given the shortage of matrons, the children were largely responsible for looking after themselves and each other. When Sister Jane did travel to the Generalate to ask that more sisters be sent to Mercy House, she was brushed off. To make matters worse, a few days later she received a letter asking her to teach two days a week as part of a collaborative vocational training school arrangement. Sister Jane had gone to ask her superiors for more staff, and they responded by giving her another task.

The problem of understaffing acutely affected Mercy House's residents. Many of them told me they felt the sisters no longer had time to listen to their problems or to counsel them, and they longed for someone they could talk with freely. This issue was especially important for some of the adolescents and young adults with degenerative illnesses, who felt condemned to watch their bodies and their opportunities slowly deteriorate. Others had lived through painful experiences of rejection, humiliation, and abuse before coming to Mercy House and felt a great need to talk with someone about their lives. One young man, Alex Lwanga, confided in me, "Listening to somebody is also another big talent. [This sister] is not a good listener at all. When you want to talk to her she says, 'I am busy, come at this time.' You wait for the time. When you go, she has so many people [to attend to]. When she comes out [she says], 'I am very tired.'" Another resident thought things had been better before Sister Caroline left: "[Sister Caroline] could also make you feel so good, she could also share the same plate with us, the way that we are." The importance of sitting close to someone, listening, and sharing food from a common plate is particularly significant given the fear of contagion that people with disabilities, especially epilepsy, often face in Uganda. One child arrived dragging a sack of plates that people had given her food on but would not take back when she finished eating. Another resident, Namuwaya Mariam, said, "What a child from here needs is [someone] to sit next to her, to touch her like the way you touched Charles, to share, so someone feels loved. Because most of them are not loved from their homes. That is the love that they are hunting for. The time given to somebody. As [Charles] was telling you, 'I feel better when someone comes and talks to me.'" Listening and physical expressions of support and solidarity were crucial to the residents' sense of being loved and cared for, a need central for many of the children and adults whose lives had been defined by rejection and abandonment.

These forms of care were also central to the sisters' understanding of charity and of the importance of their work at Mercy House to their own self-formation. Staffing decisions that favored the sustainability of the order thus made it difficult for Mercy House's residents to meet their need for support and care and also prevented the sisters from practicing the charity that was central to their charism and self-formation. In this way the Mercy House residents' complaints are fundamentally different from those made by Hope Child's participants. The Mercy House residents' demands for care were congruent with the sisters' own ethics. Rather than accusing the sisters of failing to fulfill obligations that the workers themselves opposed, as at Hope Child, the residents of Mercy House were asking the sisters to do more of what they themselves claimed they ought to be doing.

The embodied acts of care and listening that were difficult to perform given the ongoing staffing constraints are central to the sisters' understanding of their charitable work as a form of prayer and self-transformation. In a booklet on Franciscan spirituality for young women in the novitiate, Sister Reginald Gonza, who served as the Franciscan Sisters of Africa program director for the central region of Uganda in 2007–8, wrote:

> The nature of Francis and Clare's religious experiences can be said to be embodied. Whatever belongs to our human condition (joys, sorrows, weaknesses/failures, limitations, sickness and rejection) can lead us into an experience of the divine because of Jesus. . . . Francis's compassion for the marginalized (the lepers and the poor) led him to have compassion for the crucified Christ. . . . Thus the human experience with the lepers led him to experience the divine.

As I explore in greater depth in chapter 6, the sisters considered Mercy House an ideal "school of charity" because it involved the intimate work of healing wounds, filling hungry bellies, and working with people marginalized by society. The marginalized status of many of the residents was thought to offer the sisters a unique opportunity for self-transformation through participation in a chain of mimetic practice, and in this sense the sisters' daily work became a form of prayer and a means of ethical formation. The work they performed at Mercy House—teaching vocational training classes, bandaging wounds, worrying about the school fees for the many children in their care, struggling to make ends meet after accepting yet another person into the home—was an extension of the work of adoration they performed daily in the chapel.

In an article written for a self-published magazine commemorating the seventy-fifth anniversary of the founding of Mercy House, Sister Roberta Namuyiga wrote, "The residents of Mercy House are the true riches of the church in Uganda. . . . [T]hey will pass on into eternity with us when we come before the throne of God for judgment. He will point to them, saying to us, '[W]hen I was hungry, sick, naked, lonely . . . you did it to me.' The poor will be our visa into eternity. They are a treasure we must care for very well." The image of the poor beggar as a "visa into eternity" illustrates the role of charity and almsgiving in the Catholic economy of salvation. Here Sister Roberta draws on the passage from the book of Matthew in which the charitable act is not a gift made to God *through* the poor; rather, the poor themselves become figurations of God, making charity an act of adoration.

The Projects

In light of this understanding of charity, the interventions by the Franciscan Sisters of Africa were nearly the opposite of those being made by other NGOs in Uganda. Instead of holding community training sessions and working to create sustainable community institutions, the sisters focused on the direct provision of goods, services, and employment. Their activities have gone virtually unchanged since the time of Mother Mary Patrick, and they argue that moving away from providing care directly to the needy would mean abandoning their Franciscan charism, the set of teachings for their order that placed the care of the destitute at the center of their lives. The sisters' primary responsibility was seeing to the welfare of the children and adults attached to Mercy House. Concretely, this meant raising money for their school fees and other expenses, taking residents to medical appointments locally or in Kampala, visiting children in their care but living at boarding schools, and managing the poultry, piggery, and garden designed to help Mercy House achieve some level of self-sufficiency. The sisters were also responsible for managing and teaching at the small vocational school within the Mercy House compound.

In addition to the programmatic tasks that took place within the compound, the sisters managed an outside rehabilitation program staffed by two members of the local community. These two young men, James Walugumba and Chris Kaweesi, were responsible for visiting the outlying villages to identify people with disabilities and make them aware of the various treatments, medical equipment, and other programs that might make their lives easier. These people were then invited to Mercy House to meet with a doctor who regularly came from Kampala to see new patients. When appropriate, they were referred to clinics in Kampala or elsewhere where they might consult doctors who had agreed to provide free services to patients referred by the sisters.

The commercial bakery supported by the Bread for the World Foundation was also within the compound and provided vocational training and job opportunities for people with disabilities while also yielding income to fund its other operations. Camilla Korteweg, the founder of Bread for the World, told me during a 2008 interview at her home outside Amsterdam that the primary purpose of starting such bakeries was to prove that people with disabilities could work and run such a business while also spreading her love of baking bread to countries without a baking tradition. She has remained committed to both missions and insisted that all Bread for the World bakeries employ people with disabilities and that these people should hire and fire the nondisabled staff, not the other way around. She was very proud that most of the bakery employees with disabilities are now living on their own and can do things like paying their children's school fees.

Mercy House's ongoing programs were often supplemented by sporadic events initiated by people from outside the home. In March 2008 a group of British ophthalmologists made their annual visit and treated more than four hundred patients in four days, fitting many for prescription glasses that the ophthalmologists sent free of charge when they returned to Britain. During this same period, two occupational therapy students from the Netherlands created a program for six residents with severe mental and physical disabilities. These same students also financed building an accessible playground on the grounds of Mercy House.

The sisters saw all these initiatives as fundamentally different from the workshop- and advocacy-based approaches of the more mainstream NGOs.

Sister Valentine was particularly frustrated about losing the support of the British-based Mercer Foundation, one of their major funders since 1983. As I discuss in greater depth in chapter 6, in the early 1990s the Mercer Foundation altered its mission statement, moving away from direct support for operational expenses of residential facilities for people with disabilities to support legal advocacy and sensitivity training efforts. After the change, the foundation sponsored a workshop at the palatial Hotel Africana in Kampala, inviting all the people who oversaw projects it supported. "Some of the sisters were so angry about the move away from direct services that they refused to attend the event," Sister Valentine told me. "I decided to go, but I got nothing out of that workshop. People sitting around talking in a hotel has nothing to do with those in need."

Sister Valentine was similarly upset about a recent visit by the African Center for the Rights of the Child (ACRC).

> They came around collecting lots of nice stories to take back with them about all of the suffering these children had seen, but they did nothing for them! They talked so much about the importance of schooling, but did nothing to help us pay for the children's fees. Their speeches were nice, but they didn't give us so much as a little money for one blanket, yet they had 80,000 UGX (US$47) to spend on [gas for their car]. What good did that 80,000 do for us?

Sister Valentine's frustrations about the advocacy- and training-based approaches of other NGOs speak to the sisters' broader opposition to the nonmaterial forms of assistance that have become increasingly dominant in the aid community since the 1990s. As noted above, many NGOs have been moving away from the distribution of material goods, or "handouts," and toward efforts to form sustainable community-based institutions and to promote advocacy and sensitization. Although these other organizations explicitly defined themselves in opposition to "charity," Mercy House saw these mainstream, sustainable program approaches as wasting money that might be spent on practical needs. For an organization like the ACRC, or for Hope Child, handing out blankets or money for school fees would be a meaningless gesture unlikely to create sustainable change, while for Mercy House failing to give concrete assistance constituted an unethical withholding of money that rightfully belonged to the residents. The sisters had little hope that advocacy would have much effect in Uganda, and they had equally little faith in the government's capacity to make changes that would actually benefit the people of Uganda. Like many Ugandans, they felt that most of the legislation passed through advocacy efforts was just "pretty words" designed to please the international community but creating little change at the village level.

Given this trend away from funding direct services, particularly those provided in institutional settings, the sisters were constantly scrambling to find money to cover the basic costs of running Mercy House. In 2008, it ran on an annual operating budget of just over 35.7 million UGX (US$21,000). This money did not come in regular installments allocated to specific budgetary categories but was pieced together over the course of the year and generally spent as soon as it came in. Approximately half of this budget was generated through the sisters' income-generating activities (IGAs), including the bakery, poultry rearing, and the piggery. The other half of the budget was made up of gifts from a few private donors, food shipments from the World Food Programme, and funds designated for the care of individual children through a Dutch foundation dedicated to the well-being of children with disabilities.

The sisters' reliance on IGAs for self-support highlights the way they shifted back and forth between making unconstrained gifts, having faith that their needs would be met through divine Providence, and worrying about sustainability and institutional preservation.[5] In November 2007 the pendulum swung toward a need to become even more self-sufficient when the sisters received an unexpected notice from the World Food Programme along with their monthly shipment of corn, beans, and nutrisoy porridge. The shocking notice informed them that this shipment would be their last. The World Food Programme had decided to shift its food aid to eastern Uganda, where harvests had been badly damaged by floods. The rains had also ruined Mercy House's cassava crop, and they were not sure how they would feed everyone until the next harvest. By spring they had barely enough food left in their storeroom to last two weeks. Their long-term goal immediately became to reestablish the gardens they had neglected since the World Food Programme started sending food, but in the meantime they put their short-term efforts into praying for a benefactor to help with their immediate needs.

Although benefactors did appear that year, none were interested in donating sacks of corn and beans to Mercy House. For example, Irish Aid contributed US$39,000 to build a new boys' dormitory. The sisters found it relatively easy to raise funds for large capital expenses like the dormitory or to expand income-generating projects, since they could justify such expenses to people interested in creating a sustainable difference. They found it considerably more difficult to finance ongoing operating expenses such as school fees, medical bills, and cleaning supplies, since people were generally reluctant to give money for things that would be consumed or used within a short time, leaving no visible evidence of their contribution. In spring 2008 the sisters and the residents were blessed with a Toyota pickup truck donated in kind from a group in Britain organized by a British Airways pilot and the team of British ophthalmologists, and with a fantastically designed accessible playground donated by students from the Netherlands, yet they could not afford the soap and basins necessary to stamp out a scabies outbreak and were forced to send children home to their relatives before the end of the term because of an extreme food shortage.

This shortage of funds for basic operating expenses was sometimes coupled with disagreements over the responsibilities of a child's relatives or benefactors, so that a child without soap might be told it was not up to Mercy House to provide it. One adolescent girl, Rosemary Namatovu, told me:

> It is hard. [The] last time I came back [with some money], but not with enough. I went to Sister and told her, "I have some problems, can you help me?" She told me, "If you want to ask for money, don't." I said, "It is not money, Sister, I need some sanitary pads." She said, "I don't have that for you." You know what I did? I asked Jesus. . . . "Jesus, I don't want to be ashamed. Once I am ashamed, you will be ashamed too. So, shift my cycle to the next month." Since then, I have gone for holiday and come back but I have not yet gone in[to] my menstruation cycle. I know [the] time will come that I will [get] it.

Struggles over who should provide such basic necessities not only reflect the limited funding for such things under the contemporary ethic of sustainability but also point to the challenges of depending on multiple benefactors.

As opposed to the shortages of the present, the sisters remember Mother Mary Patrick's reign as mother superior as a time of relative prosperity. In her efforts to expand Mercy House and the other missions she had established throughout Uganda, Mother Mary Patrick traveled throughout the United States and Europe on what she called begging tours, soliciting funds from donors and advocating for changes in the Catholic Church's teaching on appropriate work for missionary sisters. Watching the vista of Lake Victoria from Mercy House's crumbling retreat house, Sister Amelia Namukasa, the headmistress of a prestigious girls' primary boarding school run by the sisters, told me she imagined how much she would have enjoyed spending time there with Mother Mary Patrick, when everything was new and the flower gardens were blooming.

Mother Mary Patrick's success in fund-raising allowed her to distribute goods to local people with a largesse that the sisters at Mercy House found difficult to emulate. After Mother Mary Patrick's death in 1958, the Franciscan Sisters of Africa continued to receive funds from a congregation of missionary sisters she had founded in Ireland. But over time these funds dwindled and the sisters found themselves able to care for fewer and fewer residents. Sister Caroline once remarked, "That's why you hear some people say, 'Mama Patrick is not there,' because they come here for help and you say, 'I don't have [any],' and they say, 'Mother used to give things to the people. Mama Patrick used to give blankets. Mama Patrick used to do this.' Mercy House was known [for letting] anybody . . . come here and get what he or she needs, people were coming, when you feel you are needy you just come [to] Mercy House. So they don't know that [we] don't have." The sisters' inability to match the generosity of Mother Mary Patrick was a concern that differed markedly from the Hope Child staff's complaints that the people of Sebanda had been made dependent by the giving of previous NGOs. For the sisters, it was not that the requests and complaints were unreasonable; rather, they lamented their own inability to respond adequately and complained that donor priorities were part of the reason for their financial problems.

The Needy

In 2008 Mercy House was responsible for fifty-two children attending primary school, forty-seven teenagers attending secondary school, twelve young adults attending university, twelve vocational training students, eleven teenagers with severe mental or physical disabilities, and ten elderly residents. The sisters saw all these people as "needy." They regularly distinguished between the poor and the needy. "Most people in Uganda are poor, but few are truly needy," Sister Caroline told me. "We are here to help the truly needy, those who would not be able to do for themselves if we were not here." Being needy meant being at the bottom of society with nowhere else to turn for support. While the category of "the needy" persistently resists formal definition and measurement, the stories Sister Caroline and Sister Jane told brought this fuzzy category into focus. Pointing to a boy who looked about thirteen years old, Sister Caroline said:

That one, Malembe, his mom died when he was two and he went mental. His father was one of our cooks and he would bring that boy with him every day and lock him in the storeroom. One day the father left and didn't come back. Three days later we found the boy in the storeroom. He had nearly starved! . . . We decided to keep him in the [building] where the cow is sleeping now and feed him from there. But when we let him out he would run away. . . . Eventually we decided to take him to Butabika [the national psychiatric hospital] because we couldn't manage him here. When he returned, he was much better. . . . But his father still refused to take him back. . . . We got [the father] to agree to take Malembe with him during the day while he collected firewood [in the forest] for [us] . . . and then [Malembe] could sleep here at night. . . . The father left with the boy, but that night he returned the boy and never came back. We decided after that to keep him here at Mercy House, but the elderly objected, saying that he was stealing their food, which he was, and that Mercy House was for the old and the lame and the orphans, not for the mentally disturbed. I told them that he had every right to be there. The elderly would beat him and throw stones at him, but we kept him anyway. One day when we were at [the psychiatric hospital] for a follow-up visit, we received word that Malembe's father had died, and we quickly came home to attend the burial. . . . All of the relatives refused to take care of the boy because of his mental problems. I told the elders that now that the boy was a full orphan, they couldn't refuse him a place at Mercy House. I told them that they didn't have to like him, but that they shouldn't beat him and should let him be in the compound. He is now living here and is doing a bit better.

Malembe's story demonstrates not only the complexity of the "needy" category, but also the tensions between the various residents of Mercy House.

Many of the needy children at Mercy House underwent a period of rehabilitation and were then enrolled in formal education so they could eventually become self-sufficient and leave Mercy House. But for some like Nelson Nsereke, a young man suffering from severe hydrocephaly, self-sufficiency was not considered possible. And yet even in this case, the sisters trained and educated a sibling to act as a caregiver. The sisters envisioned ultimately being able to move them out of the home together once the sibling had received enough education to get a job that could support them both. In this instance the sisters' practices reflected a logic of sustainability, but one focused not on the sustainability of an organization or an institution but on the sustainability of a person, or in this case a pair of people. By dealing with both the resident and the caregiver, they were assuming that the pair would remain committed to one another and hoped this commitment could be encouraged by the caretaker's experience of receiving assistance, as discussed below.

The priority given to helping the needy at Mercy House contrasts with Hope Child's focus on self-sufficient strangers. While the sisters expected everyone to participate in running Mercy House and asked residents' relatives to contribute to the upkeep of their kin and the Mercy House community, the residents' did not have to show potential or participate in events to be included, and their families' contributions varied widely. Intake decisions also demonstrated little concern for the impact an incoming resident might have on the well-being of the existing residents. Whereas staff members at some of the other children's villages I visited in Uganda emphasized the challenges they faced in selecting new residents from long lists of eligible orphans, the sisters at Mercy House were hesitant to turn anyone away, despite the costs and overcrowding. Rather, they looked at the prospective well-being of the children in question. If they thought they would fare better at Mercy House than if they were turned away, the sisters tried to find some way to take them in. By contrast, many other children's villages in Uganda look primarily to the well-being of the children already in their care. The best-interest standard of those already enrolled provided a compelling moral compass, while those outside the gate aroused no sense of obligation. Within the ethics of charity, any child in need was worthy of the sisters' concern, regardless of their capacity to maintain a certain standard of care. No one in need was excluded, leading some American and European volunteers at Mercy House to worry that the sisters were bringing in more children than they could care for. "They continue to take in children without thinking about whether there will be money to feed them and send them to school," one protested to me.

The sisters' limited funds and the many people they found themselves responsible for compromised their ability to match the care given in better-financed children's villages, places I often thought of as housing an emerging class of "orphan elites." While the children at Mercy House had food and clothing, a place to sleep, and school fees, they lived like the other village children in their standard of living and in largely relying on one another for care and attention.

Ethical Assemblages

A primary goal in this chapter is to show how Mercy House and its particular forms of care have emerged from the interaction between Catholic ideas about charity and two distinct Kiganda ethics of interdependence: *omutima omuyambi* and patronage. I have found it helpful to think about this unstable confluence of ethical forms as an ethical assemblage. If, following Foucault ([1977] 1980), we can think of an apparatus as a heterogeneous collection of discursive and nondiscursive elements coming together around a particular problem at a specific historical conjuncture, we can think of an assemblage as a less stable network that has not yet stabilized as an apparatus (Deleuze and Guattari 1987; Li 2007; Ong and Collier 2005; Rabinow 2003; Zigon 2011). This way of thinking about the emergence of ethical forms emphasizes the absence of a single coherent logic, allows us to think about both discursive and nondiscursive elements, and lets us consider how these elements rearticulate themselves in relation to one another over time. It will become clear that this shifting and rearticulation can also take place on a smaller scale, with certain elements emphasized by certain people in particular situations.

Unlike the situation where the staff of Hope Child and the residents of Sebanda were operating within different assemblages that came into frequent conflict over issues of interdependence and reciprocity, here at Mercy House the residents and sisters shared the same ethicomoral assemblage. This is not to say that they all espoused exactly the same values and practices. They differed in access to resources and influence as well as in the intensity and intentionality of their commitment to Christianity, which varied among the residents and the nuns, and significantly altered how individuals related to various elements of this assemblage. Yet despite these differences, a shared moral world made the actions of the nuns and the residents mutually legible.

Having Heart: Charity and Mutima

There is a certain kinship between the Kiganda concept of *mutima* (heart) and the Christian notion of charity embraced by the Franciscan Sisters of Africa. In discussing charity and *mutima*, Sister Jane used nearly identical definitions and concretely linked them, saying:

> The practice of charity means giving without expecting a reward or payment from the one you are offering the service; in other words, it means free service given to a person in need. What we are doing at Mercy House is a form of charity. . . . Me, as a Muganda, I think the practice of charity or caring for the poor relates to the Baganda idea of *mutima omuyambi*, or heart for helping, because this means giving freely without any strings attached.

In Sister Jane's description, both charity and *mutima* are defined by their lack of reciprocal exchange. In both, gifts are given "without expecting a reward or payment" or "without any strings attached." What separates *mutima* from other forms of assistance is its lack of reciprocal obligation, and this was repeated by many people when I asked about the concept of *mutima*.

The slippage between charity and *mutima* was even more direct in other conversations where people moved easily between Kiganda and Christian idioms. In an e-mail exchange with my host father, Evarist Musumba, he replied this way to my questions concerning Ugandan experiences of receiving help from abroad:

> When Ugandans get help people from outside . . . [it] is highly valued, it is even valued better than help from their relatives or neighbors. Just imagine, a person who is not a relative and she or he is thousand miles away [and wants] to help them! It is a real sacrifice. But all my explanations . . . are centered on the word *mutima*. Viewed in the context of Uganda, *Okutwalira awamu abantu abalina omutima omulungi bayamba abantu abalala oba babamanyi obatebabamanyi*. In English it means, "Generally, people with a good heart help others whether they are known to them or not." It is even written in the Holy Bible that if you give something to another person, God pays you back more.

Here Musumba's response includes the ways distance indexes how much a gift can be considered a "real sacrifice" and the subsequent "value" assigned to that gift by its Ugandan recipient. At the end, he shifts between the idea that people with a good heart make gifts to others whether they know them or not and an unspecified biblical promise that God will repay those who give such gifts.

Comments like these raise the question whether this particular usage of the word *mutima* was, in fact, not an element of precolonial Kiganda ethics but rather a syncretic invention accompanying the introduction of Christianity in Uganda in the last quarter of the nineteenth century. Yet the nostalgia of people who mourned that "the heart of helping collapsed long ago" and Sister Jane's assertion that charity and the Baganda idea of *omutima omuyambi* were related but not identical suggest that *omutima omuyambi* is locally conceptualized as an indigenous moral virtue.

Making Obligations: Charity and Patronage

In many cases the Franciscan Sisters of Africa at Mercy House took in children and other people they did not know, some left at their gate without so much as a name. In other cases the sisters were caring for children whose parents had sought them out because they knew they would became unable to care for their children themselves. One afternoon Sister Jane described to me how one child's mother established a relationship with the sisters.

> When I was a novice in the formation house, [Tamusanga's] mother used to come with the children. . . . That mother would come, she had rashes all over, they had not yet started with those ARVs [antiretroviral medications used to treat HIV/AIDS]. She would come to beg [for] food every lunch and [she] would bring us [banana] leaves [for steaming *matooke*]. . . . But now when we finished, we professed and that lady died and had nowhere to take the children . . . the last two, Tamusanga and [his] sister [Harriet], they were brought to this home.

In this story we can see Tamusanga's mother cultivating a relationship with the nuns of Mercy House through a series of requests, a way of establishing a bond of patronage so that some of her children might be cared for after she died.

In other cases the sisters' obligations to particular children had been established through relationships built on labor as might have traditionally been found between patrons and clients in Buganda. As I described in chapter 2, chiefs appointed either by the *kabaka* or by the clan leadership had an obligation to care for those who farmed their land or labored at their request, and these obligations of care extended beyond the period of service provided the client did not leave in search of another patron. It was in this way that children like Paul Kasirye, whose father had worked as the sisters' driver, and Nalungu Margaret, whose mother had been one of the cooks, had come under the care of the sisters. When the parents died, the sisters felt obligated to care for the children they left behind. Similarly, Temba Charles, one of the boys the sisters chose for inclusion in an American-run sponsorship program they administered, secured his place based on his desperate circumstances: he had been living with his grandmother, who suffered from a heart condition and was also HIV-positive. Yet Temba Charles's place on the roster was also ensured through his grandmother's bond of obligation with the sisters because of her long-standing employment in the novices' kitchen garden. Though she was no longer able to work, the sisters felt an obligation to her family, so they built her a burned-brick house with a sheet-iron roof and secured a sponsorship for her grandson.

Holly Hanson describes how British colonists and missionaries failed to understand the nature of these obligations, both that one's obligations to one's workers exceeded the bounds of contract and that requests themselves were a sign of love that bound the giver to future gifts. In one passage Hanson describes how a young Muganda man was disappointed by the Protestant missionary C. W. Hattersley's refusal to give him money to pay bride wealth after he had worked in the man's household for nine years. According to Hanson, the young man protested, "When I came to join your establishment I gave myself entirely to you. Since that time you are my father; I have no other. Were I to apply to my father, he would only refer me to you. . . . [Y]ou altogether fail to understand the customs of the Baganda. Do you not know that the more requests we make the more we show our love for you? Were it not that I greatly love you, I would never ask for a single thing" (Hanson 2003, 7).

From the perspective of Maussian reciprocal obligation, the young man's first claim is fairly easy to comprehend. In exchange for the gift of service, Hattersley ought to have recognized the extracontractual relationship that had been formed and reciprocated by helping the young man pay bride wealth. The second claim, that "the more requests we make the more we show our love for you," is more difficult to understand but is essential for comprehending how Tamusanga's mother arranged long-term care for her son. In this second claim we hear the ways that making and fulfilling requests create an obligation for the giver to give again. These gifts may be answered or prompted by reciprocal gifts, but normally it is the prior giving, not the prior receiving, that creates the obligation for future gifts. In contrast to Marcel Mauss's framework ([1925] 1990), which focuses on the agency of the giver and the potential shame of being a recipient, within this ethically viable framework asking and receiving constitute an agentive act that asserts one's love for the prospective giver and positions both giver and receiver as equally agentive (Durham 1995). It also establishes a particular form of intersubjectivity by communicating aspects of one's personhood to others (Klaits 2010, 2011).

In line with this, we can see the agency in some of the Mercy House residents' active pursuit of the sisters' patronage. For example, Sister Caroline first met Namika Rebecca near the Martyr's Shrine just outside Kampala on Martyrs' Day. Namika was then in primary five. During an interview in June 2010, Namika told me this:

The sisters were so beautiful dressed all in white and smiling. I was immediately drawn to them. They asked me where I lived and I pointed to a house nearby. They asked me if I had my dad; I said that he had died. They asked me if I had my Mom, and I said yes. [They saw the condition I was in and] said that they wanted to take me to Mercy House to go to school. I was very excited about this idea and went home and told my mother. My mother re- fused and kept me at home. When I was nearing the end of [primary seven], I went to my mother and asked her what her plans were for me. She said she was planning to put me in tailoring. I said that I didn't want to do tailoring [and] that I wanted to [do] academics and that I was leaving to go to the sis- ters so that they would send me to school. I traveled here and started school across the way at Saint Anthony's. There was another school they might have sent me to, but it wasn't so accessible. This was a real blessing since Saint Anthony's has better academic standards. I [worked very hard on] read[ing] and eventually scored a nineteen out of twenty-five on the A-level exam and am now just waiting to hear about my university placement.

People in Uganda have long used multiple patrons as resources for achieving their goals. In a similar fashion, Namika saw the presence of Mercy House and the sisters' offer of an education as allowing her to make own choices about her life plans and to pursue her academic goals. While depending on the sisters was not without its challenges, accepting their charitable gift created more options for Namika.

When God Makes You His Messenger

The parallel logics of Catholic charity and indigenous forms of patronage are doubled in the ways Catholic charitable givers, Baganda or otherwise, understand their relationship with God.

Owing to the shortage of sisters and paid staff, the children and other residents of Mercy House largely looked after themselves and one another. During one of my visits, I slept in a guest room attached to the boys' dormi- tory. Early each morning I was awakened by the sounds of the boys mop- ping the floors of their dorm and directing one another as they got ready for the day. Boys with disabilities had trouble with some tasks, so other boys helped them, and they in turn helped others. During my interviews with the residents of Mercy House, I often asked them about these relation- ships built on mutual aid. Fred Lukomwa, a young man who had a mobil- ity impairment, told me this:

FRED: I give [other children] help like, tell[ing] them to bathe, washing [their] clothes, taking care [to see] whether they have got[ten] food.

CHINA: What motivates you to do this?

FRED: In the hospital [a lot of] people [gave] me care. Because my brother was young, he could not manage to take care of me. But different people helped me. And, in addition to that, doctors who worked on me were from different countries. Bas[ed] on that, I see that really I have to help as a reward to those who helped me. I will never be able to help those people and so I help [the boys] instead.

CHINA: Do you expect anything from the people that you help?

FRED: No.

CHINA: Do you expect anything from anyone else?

FRED: Except from God.

CHINA: Do you think anything might happen to you because you help others?

FRED: Of course. You never know the blessings. Perhaps I may die [tomorrow] but according to what I do, maybe God [extends] my days for being a good person.

Fred did not expect to benefit directly from those he was helping, nor did he feel obliged to directly repay those who had helped him in the past. Rather, he helped the other children in the dorm to reward those who had helped him when he was in the hospital and to secure future blessings from God.[6] These ways of conceptualizing the expected rewards of giving challenge more simplistic understandings of gift debt, which see the recipient as bound to make a return gift to the original giver.[7] This constant flow of mutual aid also unsettles assumptions that these children see themselves only as objects of pity and recipients of assistance. To the contrary, Fred's comments reveal the ways caring for one another created spaces where the children were both givers and receivers of charity.

Nakatana Kizito, a devout charismatic Catholic from Sebanda, described his charitable gifts in a similar fashion when I interviewed him with my assistant George in June 2010. Kizito's father, who had almost joined the seminary, had raised him as a Catholic, but as an adult Kizito had turned away from the church. When the Catholic charismatic renewal movement started to take hold in Sebanda in the mid-1990s, Kizito returned to the church. The profound religious experience he attributes to the Catholic charismatic renewal led him to give up drinking and growing sugarcane for distillation, and he started attending morning mass daily at the Sebanda parish church. Kizito was also redistributing some of the money he had made from his restaurant Kisa Kya Maria (Blessings of Mary), which he opened about the same time he returned to the church. Kizito concentrated on the elderly, supplying milk from his cows every day. He gave milk to people like Simon Nanda, an elderly man who lost the use of his legs in a bicycle accident, and whom he saw as in particular need. Nanda receives little assistance from his grown children, who resent his lack of care for them during their youth. He regularly drank locally distilled alcohol, depleting the family's meager resources and frequently becoming violent. In his old age Nanda had stopped drinking, but he could not mend his relationship with his estranged sons, who refused to care for him and even stole the little money he earned selling beds and dish racks he fashioned out of cane and nails. Nanda found himself dependent on charitable gifts from people like Kizito and the nuns and priests of the local parish. Kizito saw the elderly, in particular, as in special need of care and attributed his helping them to his renewed interest in religion.

KIZITO: For me, I just give the tenth [of my income]. The Bible, in Malachi, it says that, "You cheated me of offerings and the tenth." So if you don't give offertory, you cheat God. He says "bring offerings and the tenth." That is what I do, and if we went to the farm I would have shown to you that "these banana plants are reserved for the Lord." I don't eat them. If I harvest them, I take them directly to the church. It is different with the people. That also is in the Bible: "When you went to the hospital and visited the sick, you visited me. You gave to the poor and you gave to me." That differs from the tenth. When I get out of the church, I go and visit the sick. When I get back home, I pray for them. That is what was written; when you visit the sick, you do it for Jesus. God may not reward you directly, but there are things that he can get you through. To [have a] friendship with God is the biggest treasure one can have. I will give you an example. When I give [to] you and you don't give back to me, we . . . have created a bond. You start loving me, even when you . . . don't give [to] me. With my friendship with God, I pass through many hardships. He says that "call me and I will answer" because he is just near you. I take it as the president is to his ministers; he can plead for one of them when he commits an offense. That is exactly my relationship with God, when I fall in any hardship, I call his name.

GEORGE: [It is like] In this CHOGM[8] scandal the president came out and saved some ministers, yet they are totally guilty; because they are friendly with him.

KIZITO: Because they have a relationship. [A government minister] tells him that "I confess to have stolen the money but please bail me out". When the president says . . . "Leave him," they do so. Likewise when I commit an offense, the angels can easily bail me out because of the good things that I may have done. I may easily pass where you can't. The scripture about Daniel says that he was put in the lions' den, wanting them to feed on him. And it is said that they had starved the beasts for days. But [the lions] never touched him because of his relationship with God.

Kizito's thoughts on charity draw on the figures of master and servant, figures essential to the precolonial ethics of patronage and inequality. He believes that the people God chooses as his servants are protected in much the same way that President Museveni protects his ministers, an image he associates not with corruption but with the proper state of relations between patrons and clients. Speaking of his own experience and pointing to a painting of the Virgin Mary on the wall of his restaurant, Kizito attributed his success, which had allowed him to buy a blender and to add a shaded veranda to the front of his restaurant, to Mary's patronage, which he links to his patronage of others.

Kizito is a patron to the people he visits and brings milk and other material goods, yet he also considers himself God's messenger and servant. Baganda, and anyone who becomes involved with them, are generally expected to occupy a position in the hierarchy of mutual obligations, which makes them patrons of some and clients of others. Charitable exchange complicates this hierarchy, because the charitable gift makes one *simultaneously* an earthly patron and a heavenly client.

Charity's Wounds?

The idea that charitable gifts are actually exchanges with God is just one of several points that raise questions about Pierre Bourdieu's arguments on the symbolic violence of charity. For Bourdieu, charity was the primary example of the symbolic violence he spent his career writing about. In his words, gifts are nothing more than the "endless reconversion of economic capital into social capital." Since "wealth . . . can exert power, and exert it durably, only in the form of symbolic capital," gifts become one of the primary ways the wealthy control people. Gifts thus function as "ideological machines [that perpetuate the] unequal balance of power." Bourdieu argues that this is all made possible by a collective misrecognition in which both giver and receiver see gifts as "exaltation of gratuitous, unrequited generosity" (Bourdieu 1977, 192). Bourdieu claimed that this misrecognition is facilitated by the obligatory time lapse between gift and countergift. Bourdieu argued that in his commitment to a synchronic structuralism,

Claude Lévi-Strauss failed to see the critical importance of the timing of the gift and the way delayed or impossible reciprocation took an extended toll on the recipient by perpetuating unequal relationships (192–97).

Yet when we suspend our reliance on misrecognition and look more closely at the experiences of givers and receivers of charity, we find that Bourdieu's argument concerning the *necessary* violence of charity is questionable. Historian Holly Hanson is similarly suspicious of Bourdieu's argument:

> Baganda . . . would have taken issue with Bourdieu's assertion that recip-
> rocal exchange is always symbolic violence. . . . To assert that "gentle, hid-
> den exploitation is the form taken by man's exploitation by man whenever
> overt, brutal exploitation is impossible" (Bourdieu 1977, 192) naturalizes
> domination and makes it inevitable. This perception impedes our capacity
> to recognize forms of power that may not have been coercive, and erases
> the possibility of non-oppressive relationships in the past or in the future.
> Humanity's capacity for moral choice is lost in a teleological expectation that
> human beings have always oppressed or been oppressed, and that only a
> future reorganization of social and political structures will create conditions
> for production characterized by moral interaction. It is more complicated,
> but perhaps more useful, to acknowledge that a particular habit of thought
> or social institution can at times oppress and at other times empower. (Han-
> son 2003, 15)

Hanson's argument opens a discussion of the contingency of the gift: Sometimes it is exploitative; sometimes it is not. Taking a nominalist stance, she urges us to pay closer attention to the use particular gifts are put to rather than assuming universal motivations and outcomes. Denouncing universalizing tendencies is far from original, yet Bourdieu's arguments regarding the wounds that charitable actions necessarily inflict continue to influence popular and anthropological critiques of charity.

While not excluding the possibility that giving to charities increased the social capital of Mercy House's donors, we must attend to the ways the ethics of inequality work in Buganda. It is not inequality itself that is the problem, but what people do from their positions within the hierarchy. Being elite is not considered a problem as long as one is a generous person who properly observes the injunction to redistribute wealth. By not taking his Kabyle informants at their word when they say, "The rich man is rich so as to be able to give to the poor" (Bourdieu 1977, 195), Bourdieu failed to see this as an alternative ethical framework. Instead, he focused on the inequality produced through unrepayable gifts in "archaic societies." Such a view relies on a sense of "misrecognition," which allows only the anthropologist the privilege of seeing the truth behind the mask. This view also minimizes the experiences of the recipients, who have long found gifts made through logics of patronage or charity to be an effective means of climbing the social and economic hierarchy.

In addition, Bourdieu's characterization of charity reduces God's role as the recipient and presumed reciprocator of Catholic charity to a superimposed illusion that hides the self-interested nature of charitable gifts. Yet when we resist a hermeneutics of suspicion, Kizito's claim that he gives to the elderly in his village as a way to give to God, both as a gesture of gratitude for the unrepayable gift of salvation and as a way of soliciting his protection—a claim echoed by the sisters and their donors—raises questions about the effects of this belief. For Kizito, God is his primary exchange partner, so his return of gifts from others, even intangible ones like loyalty or respect, are at most secondary to this spiritual motivation. If we follow the anthropologist Jonathan Parry in his critique of interpretations of Mauss that overemphasize the importance of earthly reciprocity (Parry 1986) and open the question of spiritual modes of exchange, we are left with some interesting but as yet unanswered questions about the forms and effects of "gift debt" created through charity.

Bourdieu's argument attempts to separate "self-interested gifts" from "true gifts" and thus fails to understand Mauss's primary point that before the creation of the market there was no distinction between interest and disinterest; they were not opposites joined in a paradox but coexisted in an problem-free union. The same was true for the ancients, who saw right action not as in conflict with their own self-interest but as ultimately leading to a flourishing life. The separation between self-interest and altruism found in Malinowskian interpretations of Mauss, which focus on the strategic actions of self-interested actors, blinds modern readers to the inseparability of these categories both in Kiganda ethics of patronage, in which the patron has a moral obligation to take on additional clients if he is able and personally benefits from doing so, and in Catholic ethics of charity, in which the giver has a moral obligation to give to God by giving to the poor and may expect otherworldly benefits from doing so.

Even though Bourdieu's claim that charitable gifts fail to overturn structures of inequality seems consistent with my data, that is not the whole story, since certain forms of charity and patronage do result in significant socioeconomic mobility. In Uganda, where only 4.5 percent of adults have completed secondary school (Uganda Bureau of Statistics 2002), the charitable scholarships provided through institutions like Mercy House, which in 2007–8 paid school fees for forty-seven secondary school students and twelve university students, constituted a critical point of access to higher education. In addition, a national study exploring factors that contributed to social mobility similarly found that strong religious, personal, or family networks were among the most important predictors of social mobility in Uganda (Ministry of Finance 2007). And while poverty and inequality are not the same thing, at a more fundamental level Bourdieu's problematizing of inequality is in many ways foreign to Uganda. In Uganda it is not dependence and inequality themselves that are considered a problem; rather, it is what one *does* from one's position within a given hierarchy that is the focus of moral anxiety.

This is not to say that the residents of Mercy House did not have complaints. But most of the residents said they preferred life there to the difficult conditions they had left behind, even though many still missed their families. Alex Lwanga pointed out this nuance, saying, "Well, anywhere one lives which is not their home, even when everything is there, it can never be better than home. And so this place is good but home is better, seeing and chatting with them. But we do not want to leave, as you may know, the conditions of Mercy House [are better]. That is [why] this place is preferred."

Boredom, for example, was a major complaint for children. Some complained about the lack of a structured program or opportunities to play sports such as football or netball. Others complained that the sisters would not let them watch enough of the television donated by a pair of Dutch volunteers. Charles Ayesiga, a young man who was bedridden by a degenerative disease, simply wanted to listen to his small radio, which often had dead batteries. He said, "I am not happy when I do not have a radio. I [often] feel bored. If I have my radio with me, I feel nice. But if I do not have anybody to chat with, I feel very [sad]." Fighting among the older girls was another source of stress and anxiety for many.

These complaints voiced in my interviews with the residents of Mercy House reveal that the sisters' charity places them in a better position than they left behind, but that they remain vulnerable to the rules and demands of those they depend on. Most, if not all, children find themselves in this situation as dependents, which perhaps explains why it was the young adults who were most likely to bristle at the sisters' constraints. In regard to the larger argument of this book, many of the Mercy House residents' thwarted desires pertain to the need for more charity rather than less— more batteries for radios, more money for transportation home, more basic supplies like soap and sanitary napkins. Yet at the same time they point to the power dynamics in relations between givers and receivers of patronage, charity, and actions motivated by *omutima omuyambi*. The trick, it seems, is to allow these relations of hierarchy and control to remain visible while not letting their presence negate the real and much-appreciated benefits that the residents of Mercy House derive from its continued existence.

Returning to the central question of this book, attempts to "avoid dependence" are in many ways viewed as indexes of corruption, particularly in the contexts where interdependent hierarchies serve as legitimate moral forms, where those with resources have a moral obligation to take on clients, and where what I have come to see as the present devaluation of "wealth in people" is viewed by many rural people as a moral crisis. Ironically, undistributed money now pays for increasingly complex monitoring and evaluation systems, making the audit itself a form of corruption. By contrast, the unmonitored charity of Mercy House, which from the perspective of an audit culture and a depersonalized ethics of equality appears as unsustainable gifts distributed along lines of personal attachment, is often consistent with, though not identical to, the Kiganda virtues of *mukisa* (kindness) and *mutima*. In the next two chapters I shift my focus from the content of charity and sustainable development and the ways they interact to an exploration of the techniques used to instill them and to ensure that their subjects remain accountable.

FIVE

Performance Philanthropy: Sustainable Development and the Ethics of Audit

> You want to be an intelligent giver, but how can you gather enough reliable data to do a meaningful analysis? There is a simple ratio you can use in almost every giving situation to cut through misinformation or lack of information. Just as price-to-earnings (PE) has become a standard ratio for evaluating investments, there is also a ratio you can use in your philanthropy. It answers the question, "What is the cost of improving one person's life?" I call it the cost-per-life, or CPL, ratio. (Smith and Thurman 2007, 224)

The move toward participation, sustainability, and community ownership at the turn of the twenty-first century was directed at least in part by a desire to increase aid effectiveness. In line with increasing returns on philanthropic investments, both large and small donors operating within this development paradigm have become more concerned with seeing the impact of the money they donate. This mode of normative decision-making relies on NGOs' having the capacity to produce visible, often quantitative, proofs of their outcomes. These outcomes are then read against project expenses, and the resulting figure serves as a key measure of programs' success and fundability—as we see in the cost-per-life-changed ratio championed by the philanthropic advising firm Geneva Global. These ever-increasing demands for quantifiable proof of success reflect global trends toward audit as a mode of ensuring accountability and ethical conduct (Power 1997; Strathern 2000). This method for ensuring accountability is fast becoming the dominant ethical framework in contemporary development work.

To comply with this ethical mode, NGOs like Hope Child have now developed internal monitoring and evaluation (M&E) departments dedicated to producing and collating reports and internal studies (Bornstein, Wallace, and Chapman 2006). Bureaucratic writing and statistical documenta-

tion play an important role in the composition and governance of populations (Foucault [1977] 1990, 2007; Scott 1998). In addition, these legible
forms of bureaucratic practice often constitute structural violence through
the "social production of indifference" (Herzfeld 1992), allowing "grave
national cris[es]" to become "unexceptional, a matter of routine administration" (Gupta 2012, 22) and making state bureaucrats indifferent to the
outcomes of their myriad programs, regardless of the noble intentions or
motivations of those the state employs (Gupta 2012). While such insights
are important for understanding how qualitative and quantitative forms of
record keeping constitute and shape the conduct of the populations that
Hope Child defined and managed through their programs, here I want to
explore these forms of accounting from a different angle. In turning my
attention to audit in this chapter and to virtue in chapter 6, I shift my focus from the roles of dependence and gifting in the ethical assemblages of
sustainable development and charity to how actors involved in these assemblages think about questions of accountability and ethics. In doing so
I attend to how these particular instantiations of utilitarianism and virtue
ethics differ in their understanding of how ethicomoral codes ought to be
implemented, the role of discipline and subjectivation within these theories, the forms of thought and action that are enabled or foreclosed, and
the ways these different forms of ethics and governing shape the sort of
projects that can be implemented.

Through my analysis of technologies of audit, I demonstrate the central
role played within this ethical form by the acquisition of the skills necessary to produce documents that meet a stringent set of formal criteria. In
this system it is documents that are saturated with power and meaning,
while the agents who create them are seen as essentially interchangeable
provided they have acquired the skills to complete the task successfully
(Poovey 1998, 42). At the same time, audit provides a set of panoptic disciplinary techniques, such as those Foucault (1978) described in *Discipline
and Punish*, through which subjects know they may be watched and so learn
to watch themselves (Poovey 1998, 60). This self-monitoring may result in
clever games designed to meet the technical demands of the audit (Brown
2010), or it may alter the behavior and beliefs of the disciplined subject at
a more profound level. In addition, I describe how in certain circumstances
employees involved in systems of audit enthusiastically learn these techniques of self-monitoring with the aim of marketing themselves for other
work in a philanthropic field that requires fluency in the language of audit.
What is at stake in these projects of entrepreneurial self-making is not necessarily orienting oneself toward the good or the right, but rather enhanc-

ing one's human capital by acquiring the skills to participate effectively in the market as a human enterprise (Foucault 2008, 219–33).

In making this argument, I engage the idea of "performance philanthropy" in three ways. I first think about the demand that NGOs demonstrate the fiscal performance of their projects under the normative rationality of cost-effectiveness. At a second level, I build on Mary Poovey's (1998) analysis of the history of double-entry bookkeeping in early modern Europe to understand how organizations use precision in a range of accounting, monitoring, and evaluation practices to achieve an "effect of accuracy" and to prove their honesty and efficiency to their donors. Finally, I think about how NGO employees and volunteers use these practices to project an image of themselves as employable subjects. For this, I draw on the work of anthropologists Harri Englund (2006) and Vihn-Kim Nguyen (2010) and sociologists Ann Swidler and Susan Watkins (2009) in considering how these formalized regimes of audit serve as critical sites for self-making. Ugandan NGO employees and volunteers work to fashion themselves into modern, educated, employable subjects, leading me to attend to the aspirational pleasures derived from the experience of documentation.

Fiscal Performance

In the eighteenth century, Jeremy Bentham argued for the utilitarian principle of making decisions that would yield the greatest happiness for the greatest number of people, but the focus on "rendering things calculable in financial terms" (Rose 1999, 152) did not rise to its present importance until the 1960s.[1] After the publication of the Plowden Report in Britain in 1961, an array of new techniques and committees were created to measure the cost-effectiveness of public expenditures (Rose 1999). In the United States in the 1950s and 1960s, there first began to appear papers that explored the relevance of cost-benefit analyses for deciding weapon choice in operations research (Prest and Turvey 1965; Quade 1971). In 1961, US Secretary of Defense Robert McNamara appointed Charles Hitch as his assistant to conduct cost-effectiveness research. Hitch, who had previously been employed by the RAND Corporation, championed this new approach to decision-making. By 1965 President Lyndon Johnson was so pleased with the results of cost-effectiveness analysis within the Department of Defense that he demanded it be used throughout the federal government (Quade 1971). McNamara brought the gospel of cost-effectiveness with him when he became head of the World Bank in 1968.

Many have noted the consequences of McNamara's commitment to the infallibility of cost-effectiveness in terms of the human tragedies of the Vietnam War. Nonetheless, cost-effectiveness has largely become accepted as a dominant determinant of decision-making in a range of fields, including medicine, welfare, and development. There are a few voices speaking out against the potential harm of this approach as applied in medicine (Farmer 2003), but such critiques are in the minority.

Cost-effectiveness has become even more important in the age of performance philanthropy. "Performance philanthropy"—a term coined by Geneva Global,[2] a leading international philanthropic advisory firm—seeks to move beyond arithmetic comparisons between projects and instead apply the model of exponential growth of market investments to determine the outcomes of philanthropic gifts (Weiss 2007). As with conventional investing, performance philanthropists seek to maximize their returns by leveraging their investments. Central to this process is not only choosing interventions that will yield maximum growth at minimum cost, but also investing in the "organizational capacity" of nonprofits so that they can work efficiently and in ways that produce visible proof of their interventions and outcomes.

By 2008 this approach had become standard operating procedure, though its novelty can be seen in an article published in the *Harvard Business Review* in 1997. Christine Letts, William Ryan, and Allen Grossman, the authors of "Virtuous Capital: What Foundations Can Learn from Venture Capitalists," criticize philanthropic foundations for failing to invest in "organizational capacity," thus limiting the growth and sustainability of their beneficiary organizations. Though organizational capacity is never explicitly defined in the article, financial planning, back-office systems, and professional development are given as examples. In advocating for an approach to philanthropy that looks more like venture capitalism, the authors emphasize the need to focus on the demonstration of measurable outcomes and advocate for a strategy in which foundations develop five- to seven-year close mentoring relationships with a small number of organizations (Letts, Ryan, and Grossman 1997). Sustainable development projects are ideally suited to the aims of performance philanthropy because, theoretically, the local institutions created through small start-up grants may yield limitless benefits for generations to come.

The demand to accommodate this new form of philanthropy was made real to organizations like Hope Child through a series of direct requirements and training opportunities imposed by donor foundations. In Hope Child's case these requirements fundamentally changed the way it designed its programs. Lutalo Andrew, Hope Child's director of M&E, ex-

pressed the need to balance the conflicting demands for holistic programming and large numbers of beneficiaries. During an interview with me in
2007, he noted, "The program is very holistic; we are looking at [a lot of]
things. That is very demanding in terms of resources and time and we have
limited resources. . . . [S]ome people who are interested in numbers may
not be interested in the work you are doing. Many donors are interested in
numbers; USAID is very interested in numbers." The focus on nonmaterial
interventions, such as training and workshops, was one of the ways Hope
Child managed to satisfy the demand for holistic programming that is also
cost-effective. By covering a wide range of topics through low-cost training
sessions, Hope Child is able reach a large number of "beneficiaries" while
simultaneously addressing a comprehensive set of issues in a way that, with
ongoing peer-to-peer training, is both infinitely replicable and low-cost.[3]

Monitoring and Evaluation

To demonstrate its cost-efficacy and accountability, donors required Hope
Child to improve its M&E systems. To meet these demands, in 2007 Hope
Child recruited a new executive director who could specifically help the
organization improve its M&E capacity. It also created a new department
dedicated to monitoring, evaluating, and reporting on its programs, solely
in response to a requirement imposed by USAID, so that it could accept a
small grant. Between 2007 and 2009, 17 percent of the Grandparent Hope
Network budget was allocated for M&E expenses. This percentage was
slightly more than triple the proportion budgeted for material contributions to individuals or households; and the 17 percent did not include the
salaries of the executive director, the M&E staff, the time other program
staff spent compiling data and writing reports, or the M&E costs of their
funders. These unaccounted costs were substantial, since many of the Hope
Child staff members dedicated a large portion of their time to creating reports and other monitoring documents. A lot of money was spent to ensure that no money was lost.

The significant amount of time and money allocated to M&E activities
also demonstrates the importance that both Hope Child's funders and the
staff members themselves attributed to these new techniques of transparency and accountability. The growing number of firms dedicated to conducting workshops and capacity-building training sessions on M&E similarly points to the expanding need for auditors within nonprofits and for
trainers to teach people to prepare reports and other documentation for
such evaluations. By improving their M&E proficiency, Hope Child's em-

ployees proved that they made legitimate use of the grants they received and gained a significant advantage in the quest to attract future funders. Acquiring new donors is easier with compelling reports on past outcomes and mastery of crucial M&E skills.

Most of the report writing at Hope Child focused on the precise quantitative documentation of particular program outputs tied to specific objectives (Bornstein, Wallace, and Chapman 2006). Outputs were measured against specific quantitative targets, and then brief remarks were given. For example, in the first quarterly report of 2007, the staff said they aimed to "organize 30 video shows on HIV/AIDS and life skills," and their quarterly target is listed as "30 video shows." In the output column they reported that "19 video shows were held and 4,968 youths were reached in Masindi, Gulu and Apac." The remarks column clarified this: "The highest number of video shows were in Apac district where 3,237 youths were reached." The specificity of these numbers (4,968 and 3,237) is important. Their apparent precision attests to their accuracy. Although it would be impossible for anyone to verify whether 4,968 youths attended the video show, this precise number creates an "effect of accuracy" (Poovey 1998, 56), verifying the initial data collection.

I frequently encountered these reports at Hope Child's monthly staff meetings, when similar lists of goals and figures were read aloud and recorded in the minutes. The review of the minutes often took up the first hour of the meeting as people suggested grammatical and spelling changes, but content errors were rarely noted. Even at much smaller meetings, such as the one that took place every Monday morning between the two Sebanda field officers, a set agenda was followed and discussions were recorded in the minutes, because both their meeting minutes and their reports constituted artifacts that could be audited. Through these documents, Hope Child constructed a paper trail that could be checked and given to others. In this sense the minutes were not only as a record for Hope Child's own institutional memory, but also a receipt that could be checked and used for verification (Power 1997). Within the bureaucratic form, it is only through such written documentation that events can be said to have occurred (Gupta 2012, 152).

Formal M&E practices also allowed Hope Child's employees to avoid discussing many of the controversial changes that their new attentiveness to cost-effectiveness brought about. In monthly reports, and at Hope Child's monthly staff meetings, "challenges" were always listed but were rarely discussed. Problems might be raised, but they would be indefinitely tabled until the next meeting, and the meeting after that, and the meeting after that. That these challenges had been raised and duly noted in the reports and meeting minutes gave the appearance of providing an adequate response, as opposed to actually dealing with the problems. As long as they adhered to the form of the reports and minutes, staff members could effectively ignore the problems noted in the content without feeling that they had neglected their duties. The speed required to cover all the items in a standardized agenda, the reliance on checklists, and the need to produce numerous reports and presentations all worked together to prevent people from undertaking deeper analysis and addressing more troubling concerns.

For example, the first quarterly report of 2007 indicated that Hope Child intended to provide "basic household needs" such as "blankets, sauce pans, and mosquito nets" to eighty-three households, but that only four households received such support. In the "remarks" column it noted, "Fewer households were supported due to budgetary constraints." Often it seemed that the formal requirement of filling out the "remarks" column served as a substitute for discussing whether more money should have been budgeted for "basic needs" or whether some funds might have been moved into the "basic needs" line item of the budget from a line item that had not fallen short. Similarly, when a field officer from northern Uganda reported that when user fees were introduced at the Early Childhood Development center, the number of children attending had fallen by 40 percent, the act of reporting became an end in itself. There was no further discussion of whether such a steep decline required an intervention or a change in plan. The bureaucratic process of transparent reporting thus does not encourage open dialogue but forecloses it as transparency itself becomes the end product.

Capacity Building

In addition to monthly, quarterly, and annual project reports submitted by each individual field staff member, Hope Child's employees—including the cleaning person, driver, receptionist, and security guard—were required to submit personal reports each year documenting what they had accomplished. The December 2007 annual staff meeting, during which these individual reports were presented and used as an exercise to improve report-writing skills, speaks to the centrality of the bureaucratic process of report writing and presentation in Hope Child's disciplinary arsenal and to the importance of creating a staff skilled in this ethics of audit.

After reviewing the minutes from the previous meeting, the staff members were instructed to break into groups of five. Each group was given an hour to review five individual reports written by people outside the group. The executive director instructed everyone to review and analyze each of the reports and then to make a brief presentation to the whole group about what they had learned. They were asked to comment on format, issues raised, challenges faced, and lessons learned. "After you all report back, one of the officers from M&E will write a summary report based on what was reported back by those reporting on the reports."

I joined one of the groups, and we moved into an empty office to begin the task. Marline Nayiga, a social worker from the Kampala site, picked up one of the departmental reports and held it up for us all to see, flipping the pages. Most of the group members immediately agreed that the report needed a cover page. They also objected because it was written in the past tense. "The objectives and acronyms should have also been listed separately," another chimed in. "At least the figures are there; that's good."

When we reached the section on "challenges faced," the members of my group avoided discussing the actual content and instead focused on whether we should write all report challenges on one sheet. When I suggested that we might pause to discuss the challenges themselves, Otim Stephen said:

> We can just list them, there's really nothing to discuss. Late disbursements have come up a thousand times. This person probably just got their requisitions in late and that was that. Resettlement exercises in the camps were beyond his control, nothing could be learned, or managed differently the next time. Resettlements just mean that program activities had to be put on pause until things settled down.

This effectively ended the conversation, and we moved on to copying the list of challenges onto one large sheet of a presentation flip chart.

During a tea break, I asked a group of young women how they had learned to do all this report writing. Most of them had taken the same research methods class at Makerere University. Some had also taken night classes in report writing. Betty Acaya, a woman from northern Uganda who worked taking calls on Hope Child's child helpline, told me, "In both of those classes, issues of format are taken very seriously—we would be marked down and told to do it over if our report lacked the necessary components."

The presentations made when we returned to the larger group focused, nearly without exception, on format.[4] When a discussion began concerning the need to eliminate the "Hope Child contribution" line on the case-planning form, which had previously been used to note monetary or other material donations made to specific families (given that money was no longer budgeted for "Hope Child contributions"), the timekeeper jumped in, telling us to "limit the questions." This effectively closed the conversation on this topic.

At 2:30 we broke for lunch. After lunch, we were instructed to write three lessons learned, three recommendations, and three issues for discussion on sheets of construction paper that we then taped to the walls. While there were a few that pointed to concrete issues, such as the possibility of including men in the microfinance program, what a volunteer stipend should be, and whether they should register the ECD centers with the government, nearly all of the 270 pages taped to the wall asserted the need for further training in report writing, the importance of writing clear and properly formatted reports, and the need to finish reports on time.

While one might scoff at the lack of attention given to the content of the reports in favor of a focus on form, the focus on form is central to the ethics of audit. As Poovey (1998) noted, the rise of double-entry bookkeeping in early modern Europe marked a shift from attention to the status of the individuals providing the accounts or the eloquence of their speech to a stress on the formal qualities of writing. The writers then were interchangeable as long as each knew how to engage with the space of the form, which had become saturated with meaning and power (34, 42).

This focus on form is also central to contemporary philanthropic "capacity building," since the capacity for formal report production is often the purpose of capacity-building initiatives. In contrast to a case described in chapter 6, in which creating subjects capable of making relatively independent and invisible decisions is the goal of ethical practice, here the goal is producing subjects who can craft a complete and properly formatted paper trail that can be reviewed by superiors. And this becomes the central preoccupation of the staff. Even in a bureaucratic form of governance, the bureaucrat was trusted as a particular kind of expert and an impartial ethical subject, able to make decisions in relative isolation according to a set of rules (Power 1997; Weber 1978). These new regimes of audit, by contrast, focus on developing a subject able to produce documents that theoretically allow for constant checking by others, effectively eliminating the need for trust (Power 1997).

In addition to its attempts to "build capacity" among its paid staff, Hope Child also sought to increase the documentary abilities of its volunteers. In light of this, the village volunteers responsible for coordinating the

ECD centers, youth clubs, and Grandparent Hope Network support groups were also trained in M&E practices. These individuals were responsible for keeping meticulous records of their groups' activities in the large hard-cover notebooks supplied. For example, the volunteer ECD center caretakers were required to keep separate files on children with special needs; the children's growth and immunizations; their academic assessments; minutes of committee meetings, general meetings, and caregiver meetings; and the financial records for the ECD centers. The teenage leaders of the youth clubs and the leaders of the support groups were also required to document their groups' activities and finances. These village-level self-reports supplemented the evaluations made by the Hope Child field staff, the Hope Child head office staff, and the employees of their funders who traveled to Uganda to tour the projects.

These village-level reporting requirements were at once a tool for surveillance and a way to "build capacity" among the village leaders. Yet given the assumption that Hope Child was going to pull out of the project after the initial three-year implementation period, after which projects were expected to continue without any outside support, what was the purpose of requiring these monitoring and evaluation skills? Were the villagers themselves envisioned as both the long-term producers *and* consumers of the program reports?

Audit is most often used when it is not possible for a principal player to directly monitor an agent's activities. Hope Child effectively served as the principal contact for the village volunteers, who then acted as its agents to the villagers. Hope Child, in turn, served as the agent for principals such as USAID and the Frans Lansing Foundation. The plans for the eventual withdrawal of support seem to make such a stress on report writing unnecessary, given the lack of a principal to whom the villagers would report in three years' time. Under the logic of "community ownership," one might argue that the villagers should have become the principals to whom the volunteers reported, a point I will return to below.

Human Capital

In thinking about the sorts of subjects the Hope Child staff members and volunteers were seeking to make themselves into when they submitted themselves to the rigors of report writing, we see that this was not only about creating "modern" or "accountable" subjects with the skills to make their actions legible to an outside auditor. It was also about creating employable, fundable subjects who, by becoming observable or legible in particular ways, thus enhance their human capital and might be able to secure permanent employment within the NGO labor market. Like the Ugandan workers who spent their evenings taking courses in report writing, village-level volunteers were also motivated to secure a position within the competitive, and relatively lucrative, NGO sector.

This process differs in important ways from the project of self-crafting that Vinh-Kim Nguyen (2010) describes in his writings on the use of confessional technologies and the production of effective testimonials in AIDS NGOs in Côte d'Ivoire and Burkina Faso. Many of the people Nguyen described, like the people I describe here, were occupied with projecting identities that might be useful in accessing scarce resources, whether antiretroviral medications or jobs within the NGO sector. In Nguyen's case, "the self" properly crafted and exposed through the confessional technologies of workshops and support groups, and translated into an effective testimonial, is the currency of the moral economy. At Hope Child it is not a testimonial based on an idea of an authentic interior self that NGO workers and volunteers hoped to trade on, but rather a concrete set of skills that would allow them to project accountability, competence, and ability to produce measurable cost-efficient outcomes to an audience of international donors. This is not to say that many of these same people did not also trade on testimonials like the ones Nguyen described, but rather that acquiring the ability to produce proposals, budgets, and reports was a distinct project in its own right.

While Hope Child ideally envisioned community members as the eventual "principals" of the project, low literacy levels among those not involved in writing the reports made these formal written reports less than useful. Instead, I suggest that despite all the difficulties of creating reports, writing them allowed village volunteers to imagine themselves as wage-earning NGO employees. Such skills are not important for managing an unfunded, sustainable community project, but they are important for someone seeking an outside donor or formal employment at an NGO. In this sense the "capacity-building" project may be essentially at odds with the idea of a sustainable community organization detached from outside funding sources. Part of the training was premised on helping village-level volunteers acquire the skills needed to become NGO employees—either by leaving the community to seek paid work in the NGO sector or by acquiring a new donor for their purportedly self-sustaining project (Swidler and Watkins 2009).

Pressure from major funders and periodic complaints about the burdensome and arbitrary nature of some these requirements (Bornstein, Wallace, and Chapman 2006; Heimer 2008) should not blind us to the internal appeal of this project of capacity building. In addition to the anticipatory pleasures such esoteric skills might provide in a search for employment, there is also some pleasure in possessing knowledge that is useful in the endless quest for marks of distinction between the precariously elite NGO workers and the "backward" village beneficiaries (Englund 2006). Finally, there are some practical pleasures to be found in report writing. A day spent at the office carefully composing and formatting a document is a day not spent trudging along muddy paths between homesteads.

While all ethical and cultural apparatuses involve some set of processes aimed at shaping subjects in particular ways, not all of them can be described as working toward subjects capable of being independent moral actors. Though we might be tempted to draw analogies between Hope Child's personal annual reports and the written examinations of conscience described by Foucault (2005), that would be a mistake. While one might argue that the reports serve a purpose similar to a confessional, creating a subject who can be trusted is never the intent. Instead, the subject created through an ethics of audit is simply one who can produce a precise written record, not one who can make strong and well-considered decisions when the proper path is uncertain.

SIX

"Let Us Make God Our Banker":
Charity and an Ethics of Virtue

It is six in the morning and raining as I walk from the concrete-floored guesthouse to the Mercy House chapel. There is no light in the sky yet; in Uganda there never is before seven. At seven the sun rises quickly, and the country will be bathed in the full light of day until the sun makes its startlingly quick descent at seven in the evening. I walk across the wet grass and along the gravel paths to the chapel. Long fluorescent bulbs light the outside of the buildings.

The chapel itself is a stately brick structure, and the floor—made of uneven red, black, and cream clay tiles—has been lovingly polished by the feet of those coming to pray over the years. Tucked into the quiet of a narrow wooden pew, I like to watch those same worshipers casually slipping off their sandals, at home with God in a house they seem to share with him. The racks on the backs of the pews hold the sisters' prayer books, many covered in worn silver foil dotted with tiny pink roses.

At the front of the church the novices, always dressed in white for prayers, lead the morning office[1] and the singing, their high voices mixing with the large Kiganda drums they play. The windows that line the sides of the church are often open, allowing light and views of the sisters' gardens to flood the space.

According to the sisters, Mother Mary Patrick was given the money to build the chapel by a stranger who appeared in front of her as she walked before sunrise one morning. As she thought and prayed for a way to find the money to build a church, a stranger appeared, handed her an envelope filled with money . . . and then vanished. The sisters have built a grotto dedicated to the Virgin Mary to mark the site. Several of the sisters told me this story nearly every time I visited Mercy House. It was also part of a formal display about the life and works of Mother Mary Patrick, assembled to commemorate the fiftieth anniversary of her death. However, in reading the few biographies that have been written about her life, I was surprised to find that this story goes unmentioned. Over time I came to see the story not only as a way of reinforcing the sisters' belief in the small miracles that they hope will prove Mother Mary Patrick's sainthood, but also as reassurance that their own financial woes would be solved. And more important, these woes would be solved not through their own planning, but through divine Providence.

Stories of the works of Mother Mary Patrick were endlessly repeated among the sisters and to me. For a long time I found their stories about their Irish foundress amusing, but they struck me as tangential to my aim of understanding the training they had gone through and the ways the order has kept tabs on them. Yet over time I came to realize that these stories were not tangential at all but were in fact the narrative to which the sisters attempted to shape themselves. It was through this process that they came to participate in what I call a chain of mimetic virtue. Within this chain the sisters attempt to transform themselves into virtuous subjects by modeling their actions on those of the saints and other holy men and women whom they see as exemplars. During their lives these exemplars also attempted to model themselves after other holy men and women. We thus find a chain of mimetic virtue extending back through the saints to Christ.

Their trust in mimetic virtue stands in place of the bureaucratic rationality of sustainable development that relies not on God's invisible accounting, but on visible ethics of audit, as described in chapter 5. Within an ethics of audit, every effort is made to render the process and results of NGO activities as transparent as possible. In this chapter, however, I describe the sisters' use of an ethics of mimetic virtue that focuses on the stories from the life of their foundress as a form of hagiography, at once didactic and deeply intimate, which helped them mold themselves to their vocations and to nurture their faith in divine Providence.

I concentrate on this distinctive way of thinking about accountability and the orientation toward time and human agency that accompanies it. By contrasting these modes of subject formation with the forms of accountability described earlier, I demonstrate how this mode of understanding accountability affected the sisters' long-term commitment to providing material charity, and how these choices made them marginal, though not necessarily aspiring, members of the international aid community. I attempt to make the sisters' actions comprehensible so that their approach to accountability can be seen not simply as a "lack" or an area where they need help with "capacity building," but as an alternative form of ethical practice.

Invisible Accounting

While the sisters of Mercy House are still able to catch the attention of the occasional one-time donor, embassy, or Good Samaritan, their refusal to engage seriously with practices of audit disqualifies them from a share of the aid that has flowed into Uganda since the late 1980s. Although those within the order at Mercy House have placed their confidence in divine Providence and the ethics of virtue, their lack of visible reports, files on residents, budgets, work plans, formal meetings, and long-term plans shocks those accustomed to working within formally managed bureaucracies and businesses. This was true both for Ugandan NGO workers and for many Western volunteers, all of whom largely embraced the regime of audit and found the sisters' lack of organization a constant source of frustration.

Monica, a Peace Corps volunteer who was finishing her two-year term at Mercy House while I was conducting my fieldwork, said that when she first arrived Mercy House was a mess, "just a jumble of people and needs." She began asking what were for her basic and necessary questions: How involved is the Board of Directors? What is the five-year plan for the home? She was stunned by their lack of answers: "These were questions that could have been pulled from a Business 101 course, and they couldn't answer them! I was ready to pack my bags and go home. I just went to my room and cried." Monica did not leave, but her frustration with the sisters at Mercy House continued throughout her stay. Despite her best efforts to "build capacity" by introducing systems, budgets, and plans, by the time she left there still was no complete list of residents or any written plan. As I tried to gather basic facts about Mercy House's operations, I too was amazed that it took me several weeks to compile a list of current residents, a task I ultimately completed by consulting several competing filing systems—all begun by well-meaning volunteers, though none were in active use—and by checking these files against the sisters' memories.

The funders they did have were those who felt comfortable placing their trust in the sisters and their training and who themselves were suspicious of other organizations and the money poured into monitoring the programs they funded. One Love, which organizes sponsorships for children attending two primary schools run by the sisters, makes little effort to monitor the use of the funds once they are wired into the sisters' bank account. Mark Daniels, the founder of One Love, told me, "I trust the sisters, that's why we work with them and not other people. Too many other programs spend too much money on monitoring and evaluation. I don't want that to happen to this program." Daniels was committed to working exclusively with nuns, since he believed their training and commitment to the work of God made them exceptionally trustworthy. He felt that neither diocesan priests nor laypeople could be trusted in this same way, given the differences in training and their ability to own private property. Camilla Korteweg of the Bread for the World Foundation, based in the Netherlands, found herself similarly drawn to the sisters' trustworthiness. Like Mark Daniels, she required little formal documentation and insisted on working exclusively with nuns.

Despite the problems the sisters faced because of their resistance to audit, one might ask if this ethical mode was necessary, not coincidental, to their ultimate aims. In *The Human Condition*, Hannah Arendt observed that Christian charity is fundamentally opposed to transparency.

> Christian hostility toward the public realm, the tendency at least of early Christians to lead a life as far removed from the public realm as possible, can also be understood as a self-evident consequence of devotion to good works, independent of all beliefs and expectations. For it is manifest that the moment a good work becomes known and public, it loses its specific character of goodness, of being done for nothing but goodness' sake. When goodness appears openly it is no longer goodness, thought it may still be useful as organized charity or an act of solidarity. Therefore: "Take heed that ye do not do your alms before men, to be seen by them." Goodness can exist only when it is not perceived, not even by its author; whoever sees himself performing good works is no longer good, but at best a useful member of society or a dutiful member of a church. Therefore: "Let not thy left hand know what thy right hand doeth." It may be this curious negative quality of goodness, the lack of outward phenomenal manifestation, that makes good works because they must be forgotten instantly, can never become part of the world; they come and go, leaving no trace. They are truly not of this world. (Arendt 1998, 74)

Here occlusion preserves purity, preventing the "good" from transforming into the "good for." In addition, the trust the sisters placed in their regime of virtue and divine accounting made formal auditing and other "rituals of verification" (Power 1997) superfluous to them. And so while the sisters often claimed to be open to learning about audit practices, they rarely made a serious effort to embrace systems that seemed redundant, and perhaps even dangerous, in the face of their existing methods for en-suring accountability. And so, whereas in a bureaucratic system of audit we find an endless regression of visible proofs, each claiming to be commen-surable with events in the world, in the sisters' ethics they place their trust in cultivated virtue and in their invisible accountability to God.

Care of the Self

Sister Amelia told me, "It is the process of formation, and the childhood that leads one to want to become a sister, that helps us to develop a strong conscience which tells us right from wrong. That is why the work we do is different from the work done by those people working at NGOs. We have a full nine years of training between the time we enter as postulants and the time we make our final vows."

Sister Amelia and the other sisters I spoke with during my fieldwork at Mercy House cited their sense of vocation and their formation period as the critical difference between themselves and their lay NGO counterparts, particularly emphasizing this time as central to their ability to "tell right from wrong." Their formation period lasts nine years, during which the sisters are shaped in many ways. In addition to the practices of labor, as-cetic self-denial, isolation, prayer, examination of conscience, and service to the poor, there are also junctures at which prospective sisters decide or are asked to leave the convent.

This idea of training and formation is very similar to exercises of charac-ter formation, or "care of the self," that Michel Foucault describes in refer-ence to the ancient Greeks and early Christians in *The Hermeneutics of the Subject* and in some of his later interviews on ethics (Foucault 1984, 1997, 2005; Rabinow 2003). These exercises in self-formation voluntarily under-taken under supervision are prerequisites for acquiring knowledge and are intended to shape a person so that personal desires align with the virtues of a particular tradition, allowing for the development of good judgment in practical matters. This preparation is an engagement of the self with the self in addition to other teachers and institutions. Through a series of exer-cises, the self becomes equipped to face future ethical challenges.[2]

The Franciscan Sisters of Africa make use of an ethical mode in which discourses, specifically their charism and Catholic theology, are instilled through specific forms of ethicomoral equipment (Rabinow 2003, 10; Fou-cault 2005; also see chapter 1), including narrative mimesis, manual labor, daily prayer, voluntary poverty, laughter, art, and frequent reassignments.

Through these forms of equipment, the sisters are formed in line with the virtues or qualities necessary to achieve the aim or *telos* of a particular practice, including, in this case, faith, humility, solidarity, and detachment from worldly concerns. A sister who has successfully undergone this formation is considered able to make decisions about specific situations in alignment with the ultimate end, aim, or *telos* of her practice. For the sisters, that end is the love of God, and all other ends are subordinate to that aim.[3]

In line with this ethical mode, a Franciscan Sister of Africa undergoes the nine-year training regime mentioned earlier. This training is preceded by a period when the young woman sill lives at home with her parents while one of the sisters guides her through a course of discernment to determine whether she truly has a calling to the religious life. If she decides she does have a calling, she may choose to explore entering into the life of the order more formally. After completing secondary school, she first spends a year living as a postulant at a remote center in eastern Uganda, where she engages in manual labor and prayer and learns about the order and about communal life. This part of the country is very hot and dry, and most sisters describe this step as very physically demanding.

After completing a year as a postulant, a young woman may choose to become a novice. After a formal ceremony during which she ritually asks to be admitted to the novitiate, she dons a modified version of the Franciscan Sisters of Africa habit and enters a year-long period cloistered in the three-story compound of dormitories and classrooms that makes up the novice house. Much of this time is spent in silent prayer and in classes. This instruction focuses on the lessons that can be learned from the lives of Saint Francis and Saint Clare,[4] and also from the life of Mother Mary Patrick. In addition to the formal education a novice receives, she is encouraged to read what she likes from the library in the novitiate. After this first year, she begins to reenter the world and is sent to spend three months working at one of the missions, of which Mercy House is one. At the end of the second year she decides whether to make the first of a series of professions in which she dedicates her life to the order. After six years most go on to make their final profession, dedicating their lives to the service of God.

Note that the sisters do not conceive of themselves or one another as blank slates. They emphasize that each sister has different gifts and talents that make particular parts of religious life easier. At times they speak of these as inborn virtues, much the way they describe *omutima omuyambi* as an inborn virtue. At other times they focus on the lessons they learned as children, from their parents and other family members. One sister recalled a class on living in community where she was taught that events experienced by a mother while she was pregnant could leave a lasting impact on the baby's character. While all the sisters make an effort to adopt a common set of virtues, there are allowances for their differences both in their assignments and in their own ways of managing the daily business of living and working together. As I discuss below, these differences can pose special challenges when sisters are assigned to work that proves an awkward match for what they see as their innate gifts.

School of Charity

In the commemorative booklet the sisters produced for Mercy House's Platinum Jubilee celebration in 2003, many sisters wrote remembrances that focused on its role as a "school of charity" through which they were better able to understand and live out their charism, or ethos of the order. It was in this spirit that Sister Pauline Atoo wrote:

> For the Franciscan Sisters of Africa, Mercy House is a window through which their charism, to love and serve the poor and the needy of our world today, is lived and practiced daily. Mercy House is the school where such lessons are learnt and shared. . . . As a living reminder of God's care, Mercy House attracts many organizations yearly, which come and perform works of Mercy or just a desire to reach others less privileged.

Sister Jean Namudosi similarly noted that until the mid-1970s, every sister who entered the formation period took her turn at Mercy House. "Having a turn at serving the poor" was seen as critical to the formation process. The training of junior sisters and novices is not primarily directed toward running programs like Mercy House, although some may eventually be sent for professional training in teaching or nursing to help them in their work. Rather, the work they perform at Mercy House is part of their ongoing development. The mundane details of teaching vocational training classes, plucking chickens, taking children to the hospital, and looking for ways to pay the children's school fees are an integral part of the care of the self. The care of the self is not the means but rather the ultimate aim of their practice. They do not seek to shape themselves so that they might better serve the poor; they serve the poor so that they might better shape themselves into true "brides of Christ." The sisters see the love and adoration of God as the pinnacle of a hierarchy of tasks. Loving God and training their souls to that end not only is the most important task, but is indeed the end to which all other tasks are but a means.

It is not uncommon for sisters to find being schooled in charity uncomfortable. While some sisters at Mercy House hoped to do this sort of work as part of their vocation, others anticipated working as teachers or administrators. While the senior sisters make some attempt to match the sisters to tasks they are best suited for, some sisters assigned to Mercy House did not want to be there. They had been sent there either because there was a shortage of available sisters or because such a placement was thought to provide an opportunity for moral growth. During an interview on her experiences working at Mercy House, Sister Elizabeth Nansubuga told me:

> I had never dreamt of becoming a social worker. . . . When I came and looked at the children, actually I didn't like it. . . . I said, "I have never had a dream of dealing with the disabled." As I grew up I knew I had a problem of being patient. I always like things fast. So it was a challenge for me. . . . I wanted to do business administration and accounts. [So] when I reached here, dealing with children wasn't easy.

Sister Elizabeth's reluctance to work with disabled people presented serious problems for those in her care. Many of the children and young adults told me that when Sister Elizabeth first arrived, she was very impatient with them and often spoke cruelly when they failed to complete their tasks. One young man confided, "We are supposed to work, but there is a way that she order[ed] us, 'Go and work there.' She use[d] much force, and when children hesitate[d], she [would remind them of the tragic circumstances that had brought them to Mercy House, revealing these stories to the others]."

The children said that over time the situation improved and that Sister Elizabeth is now more patient and kinder to them. When I asked her how this change occurred, she said:

> One day I went to the dormitory and I found Charles [a young man bedridden with hydrocephaly] on the veranda. I was with Sister Jane, and she said, "I have nobody; the boy who has been taking care of him went away. We have to clean the boy." The following day I went there and I looked at the boy and said, "Will I [do]?" It was too hard for me; to return to the boy, clean him. It was too hard, but I had to do it. When I came [back to the convent], I [did] not have appetite [for] food, but the following day I went back there and I got used to doing the work. . . . When I came here, I didn't have that

heart of taking care and really being sympathetic to the disabled children and the sick. But when you are with them, you develop it.

Sister Elizabeth's description of her own reluctance reveals a great deal about the challenges and difficulties of some types of ethical work.[5] Much like the discomfort experienced by the women Saba Mahmood described as they struggled to wake up to pray at dawn (Mahmood 2004, 124) or the shy man Pierre Bourdieu described as feeling betrayed by his own body when standing up to speak (Bourdieu 2000, 180), the actions required of Sister Elizabeth did not match her habitus, or what we might think of as her deeply embodied sense of how to perceive and act in the world, inscribed in her through her experiences (Bourdieu 1977). Setting about altering her habitus through the practice of ethical techniques, whether actively taken up or forced upon her, made Sister Elizabeth uncomfortable. In certain circumstances we might even think of using discomfort as a diagnostic for the presence of ethical work.[6] The stories the children told about how this period affected their own lives also speak to the problems this kind of ethical work can create for others who are also participants. As the superiors work to assign sisters to specific missions, they constantly must balance staffing concerns, the needs of those served by the missions, and their desire to further each sister's religious and ethical formation.

Manual Labor

Manual labor is a necessary part of the sisters' lives, and it is also deeply valued. When not in prayer, classes, or discussion with elder sisters, the novices at Mercy House spent their time carrying water, digging in the garden, cleaning, and caring for the animals. This focus on manual labor continued beyond the novitiate, so the manual tasks required to run the home competed with paperwork for the sisters' time. Sister Rosemary Nanyonjo, a junior nun working at Mercy House who was preparing to go on a six-month retreat, was enthusiastic when she described all the gardening they would do while on retreat. "Gardening is very important to the Franciscans. Even if you didn't need all of the food [for] yourself, to have some to share with the other people [is important]. And beyond that, it's good exercise and makes a person feel strong." Sister Caroline leaned back in her chair and laughed. "I was almost chased out of the novitiate because I had such a hard time waking up in the morning for prayers and didn't like carrying water. I was very fat," she said, reaching for another slice of bread. "I liked digging, but I got other sisters to carry water for me."

Most of the sisters at Mercy House looked forward to physical tasks like dressing the poultry they raised as an income-generating project. In anticipation of a Saturday of poultry dressing, Sister Valentine's face glowed with pride as she told me, "Everyone will do it together!"

Entering the compound the next morning, I saw what she meant. Everyone at Mercy House seemed to be taking part in the task of slaughtering two hundred white broilers. Those strong enough to wield axes were busy cutting off heads, while the smaller children skipped back and forth carrying the bloody, decapitated chickens by their feet to those waiting to do the next step. They handed the dead birds to the elderly people, who sat next to cauldrons of boiling water and dipped the feathered bodies in one by one to make plucking easier. The chickens were then passed to those who could not walk for the task of plucking off the feathers. Disaster, Mercy House's dog, looked on hungrily, eyeing the growing mounds of chicken innards.

Sister Caroline was seated with the pluckers, busily pulling off handfuls of wet chicken feathers. She seemed delighted to be part of the work party. Given all their unfinished grants and backlogged bookkeeping, it seemed strange to see the head of Mercy House sitting with the others plucking chickens. She looked disappointed when I, already a little nauseated from the smell of chicken innards steaming in the sun, declined to join in the fun.

Not only was raising chickens an important income-generating project; the collective labor of slaughtering them was also a form of ethicomoral training. Through collective forms of manual labor, especially messy work like slaughtering chickens, the sisters were able to enact an element of their Franciscan charism and to nurture the virtues of humility and solidarity. The morning of slaughtering chickens also allowed them to mimic Mother Mary Patrick's own manual labor. As with other aspects of their training, the sisters often remarked on her willingness to take part in manual labor and saw their own labors as modeled on hers. Public participation let the sisters demonstrate the value of work, something that Sister Valentine had stressed to me as an important part of what they wanted to teach the people living at Mercy House. During one of my first visits, she emphasized collective participation in gardening. "People learn that digging is good and see value in the food they produce and share together. Even those who crawl on their hands and knees for want of a wheelchair go to the garden to work together for an hour each evening. We all enjoy [being] together when we harvest the sweet potatoes, or roast and eat the corn together." Sister Caroline similarly stressed the importance of collective effort at Mercy House. "Everyone has to be part of the family. And when you are part of the family you must contribute, even if a smile, even if a word of advice, even if something, so that you are part, have a belonging, a sense of belonging in this family, with all the pride and confidence."

Poverty

Sister Caroline's and Sister Valentine's claims about the solidarity created through shared manual labor raise issues concerning the pragmatics and meaning of the sisters' vow of poverty. In the context of Uganda, where 31 percent of the population lives on less than a US$1 a day, thinking about what it means to voluntarily take a vow of poverty, and concretely discerning what such a vow might mean and how it might affect one's work with the poor at a place like Mercy House, is complicated. The sisters live a life that places them comfortably in the Ugandan middle class. They have electricity; bedrooms with mattresses, pillows, and mosquito nets; a generator; and regular supplies of meat, eggs, and milk. The sisters higher in the hierarchy also have running water and access to vehicles. And while they were not allowed to own property, they were given small allowances for their personal needs, which they could spend as they saw fit. Sister Valentine had been dutifully saving hers to pay for a whitewater-rafting trip at the nearby Bujagali Falls. Many of the American and European volunteers who came to work at the home grumbled about the sisters' hopes of acquiring a television, accusing them of not truly living in poverty, especially given the conditions outside their door.

What constitutes "poverty" and what purpose this vow serves have mattered deeply to the Franciscans since Saint Francis died in the thirteenth century, so much that at times the questions have threatened to divide the order. The matter was ultimately decided in favor of a more moderate reading of the vow of poverty, stipulating that although professed individuals could not own any private property, the order could (Moorman 1968). While still seeing value in living in solidarity with the poor, this moderate view also stresses that the poverty should not be so extreme as to cause great suffering. Rather, its purpose is to detach the sisters from the burdens of possessions and desire for them, which might get in the way of following their calling. In this way the Franciscan vow of poverty is more similar to the vow of obedience than to Mercy House's first Peace Corps volunteer's understanding of her own "vow of poverty": primarily learning about global poverty by living in it.

One might argue that any young woman faced with the prospect of rearing six children in a dirt-floored house with no running water might well choose to better herself by taking a vow of poverty and joining the sisters in their comfortable convent. Yet sitting among the friends and relatives of "the brides" who made their first profession in January 2008, during my fieldwork, belied my assumption that all the sisters had been facing grim village futures. While the visitors had clearly gone out of their way to wear their best clothes, the quality of the fabric used to make their *gomesas*[7] and elaborately tailored *kitengi*[8] fashions served as a ready index of the high economic status of a few of the novices' families. While many families came by public taxi, enduring the dusty two-hour journey rocking and bouncing along the rough road, others came in shiny white Land Rovers, their stylish cream suits unwrinkled and unspoiled by the dust, with some even reading the Sunday edition of the *New Vision* newspaper during the speeches made by the senior sisters and other visiting dignitaries. And so while some of the sisters increased their socioeconomic status and stability by taking such a vow of poverty, others were leaving Uganda's upper class.

The fact that they could not own private property freed the sisters from the demands of their friends and kin. "During the profession ceremony a woman's friends and relatives come to understand that none of the property of the order belongs to the sisters," Sister Amelia explained. "They learn that they cannot expect to benefit materially from their kinswoman belonging to the order." During the celebratory lunch following the profession, the vicar of Lugazi diocese mentioned that his brother was about to become the third priest in their family: "Many people are expressing their sympathy to my parents that so many of their sons had become priests." He explained that these friends believed the family would have been better off if more of their children were earning money. While the priests might enjoy a relatively comfortable life, enjoying the use of the church's property, this is not a comfort that can be shared with or transferred to their families. Thus a nun's family not only loses an opportunity to receive bride price, an issue that was much joked about in the homily during the profession mass and that has long been an issue for girls wishing to join the novitiate; they also lose the opportunity to access wealth, either licitly or illicitly, through their daughters' employment.[9]

In addition, the sisters explained that their simple lifestyle and their lack of salaries allowed more money to be spent on programs. The sisters, like many Ugandans outside the development community, were critical of NGOs. Sister Valentine lamented this over a breakfast of bread and tea one morning: "The salaries, the type of comfort those people live in, the way money is wasted at seminars at Hotel Africana!"

"It makes me sick," Sister Caroline said as we sat in her unlit office at the back of the compound, the light gradually growing dimmer and the mosquitoes buzzing in through the open shutters. "I've seen those NGO people in Lira, staying at fancy hotels, driving around in those big fuel-guzzling Pajeros. Of course those vehicles make the work easier, but it isn't the right way to go about it. When we are there, we sleep on the floor of the church with the youth. We don't stay at a hotel. We take a taxi, not a car. Instead of spending money on a hotel, we buy food which we prepare and eat together." While Sister Caroline's claims may overstate the differences between the lifestyles of nuns and of some NGO workers, she believes in the value of a simple lifestyle as an aid to instilling humility and detachment.

Mimetic Virtue

In all of these things the sisters look to their foundress Mother Mary Patrick as a model for religious life. They end each of their daily masses with a prayer of thanksgiving for her life and live in hope of her eventual beatification. During my second trip to Mercy House, Sister Jane and Sister Sylvia took me to see an elaborate exhibit that the novices made to honor the fiftieth anniversary of her death. Photographs and stories were carefully pasted onto huge display boards commemorating her life and works.

Mother Mary Patrick was born in Sligo, Ireland, in 1875. She is remembered in both a novelistic account of her life written by Sister Mary Louis (Louis 1964) and in stories retold by other sisters, now quite elderly, who personally knew her as a petite, high-spirited woman with a strong belief that God's hand was at work in the world. She seriously considered marriage at eighteen but turned down the proposal after a recurring dream in which she saw herself surrounded by dark-skinned people. "There was . . . a dark-skinned man who appeared to be someone of importance, and who kept saying to her: 'Your work is to help my people'" (Louis 1964, 12). She first thought this dream was a sign that she should work in the missions in North America, so she applied to join the Franciscan sisters at Saint Paul's Abbey in England, a newly founded order dedicated to charity work in the slums of East London and the United States. She joined them with the intention of working with African Americans. Instead she was ultimately sent to Uganda as one of six Franciscan missionaries who had been asked to join the English Mill Hill priests already there (see chapter 2 for a history of the Mill Hill order in Uganda).

During her fifty-five years of service in Africa, Mother Mary Patrick established more than thirty convents, hospitals, schools, or orphanages in Uganda, Kenya, and Tanzania. During the last years of her life, she moved to the United States but remained in frequent contact with the Franciscan Sisters of Africa. When she died in 1957, she was buried near her birth home in Sligo, but this arrangement did not last long. The *katikiro* (prime minister) of the kingdom of Buganda protested on behalf of the Catholics there, arguing, "She must come here. A chief is always buried in his own *butaka*.[10] She must be brought here for a second burial. That is the custom" (Louis 1964, 242). And so two months after her first burial in Ireland, Mother Mary Patrick's remains were disinterred and flown back to Uganda, where she was buried a short distance from the mother house in Namayumba.

The sisters made near-constant references to Mother Mary Patrick and often justified their behavior and decisions by an appeal to her actions, wishes, or intentions. The special exhibit on her life was written in a tone that suggested the miraculous, implicitly making the case for beatification. Whether or not Mother Mary Patrick is ultimately beatified, the idea that their order was founded and they themselves were trained by a possible saint, either personally or one step removed, carries great weight.

In the Catholic tradition both Jesus and the saints serve as virtuous models. For many Catholics operating within this strand of tradition, the imitation of Christ is at the foundation of what it means to lead a virtuous life. For the Franciscan Sisters of Africa, this is accomplished through the direct imitation of Christ himself and through a mimetic chain of virtue in which they model their actions on those of Mother Mary Patrick, who in turn modeled herself on Saint Francis, who in turn modeled himself on Christ.

For the sisters, learning about the life of Mother Mary Patrick by talking with the elderly sisters who had known her was an intimate form of didactic hagiography that proved crucial to their training. Sister Sylvia often spoke with great tenderness about the way she had been told Mother Mary Patrick had taught the first sisters to pray simply, "Jesus, I love you" and "Jesus, give us food." Sister Jane glowed when she spoke about Mother Mary Patrick joining the other sisters when they worked in the gardens. The intimacy with which the sisters learned the stories of Mother Mary Patrick's life was further evinced by the poetry they wrote about her and her work in Uganda, and by the brightly painted homemade papier-mâché bust of her that smiled down from a shelf in their living room.

Given the sisters' limited access to copies of the biography by Sister Mary Louis (Louis 1964) and the minor discrepancies between that biography and the stories they shared with me, it is clear that the living hagiography of Mother Mary Patrick is an intimate oral tradition in which stories are

passed from sister to sister. These stories, and not their more formal cate-
chetical training in the novitiate, were what they drew on as they worked to
mold their lives to model not only Christ but Mother Mary Patrick herself.

Providential Practices

The hand of the Lord feeds us; he answers all our needs.

—Antiphon, Psalm 145

The sisters' faith in divine Providence, their relationship with time, and
their understanding of the role of their own agency in bringing about
change in the world were among the most important results of their seeing
Mother Mary Patrick as a didactic figure of virtue. In addition to the story
of the mysterious stranger who provided the money to build the chapel,
many similar stories were compiled for the Mother Mary Patrick commemorative exhibit. Most of these stories were gathered on a board titled "Little
Miracles," and all of them featured the miraculous work of divine Providence in Mother Mary Patrick's life and in the history of the order. These
stories emphasized the virtues of prayer and faith as requisites for any accomplishment. In one, a duchess gave Mother Mary Patrick a building as a
convent for missionary sisters in Europe. In another, a midwife interested
in traveling to Africa appeared just as Mother Mary Patrick was praying for
someone to help the sisters provide better obstetric care in Uganda. These
stories echoed the sisters' own tales of providential fund-raising, since they
often narrated their own funding successes as chance encounters of divine
origin.

Laughter is also an important means of demonstrating and cultivating a
faith in divine Providence, and it was often present in the stories of Mother
Mary Patrick's life. Her biographer, Sister Mary Louis, wrote:

> Bishop Hanlon had been given a donation for the purpose of bringing a
> Community of Sisters to Uganda. When fares had been paid, outfits pro-
> vided, and a convent built, there was not much money left. At the end of six
> months the Bishop had, most reluctantly, to tell Mother Paul that he could
> no longer give any financial help towards the Sisters' maintenance; the Com-
> munity must support itself. . . . Mother Paul was stunned when she received
> the news. . . . She called Sister [Mary Patrick] and told her about this unex-
> pected difficulty. . . . Mother Paul was almost in tears as she sat down on a
> tree stump and cried: "Sister [Mary Patrick], dear, what *are* we going to do?"
> Sister [Mary Patrick] tried to find a few consoling words when, suddenly, the

ant-ridden stump collapsed and her poor Superior was left sitting flat on the ground! The situation proved too much for her bubbling mirth. She gave vent to peals of laughter. "The Bishop can't support you, Mother, and neither can the stump! We shall just trust in Providence!" The episode ended in hearty laughter, the Franciscan method of meeting a crisis, especially a financial one! They returned to the convent and, at evening recreation, Mother Paul laughingly told the Community that they were faced with utter ruin. (Louis 1964, 58–59)

Recalling such moments of laughter, the sisters continued to face crises with as much humor as possible. This is not to say they did not worry when, for example, the World Food Programme cut off its shipments of nutrisoy porridge without warning, leaving less protein for sick children. Of course they worried. But their faith that other funding would be forthcoming tempered their fear. Laughing in the face of adversity, a lesson learned by mimicking Mother Mary Patrick's own laughter, was for the sisters a providential practice through which they both demonstrated and nurtured their faith in God's ability to care and provide for them.[11]

The sisters' faith that God would ultimately solve their financial problems was also reflected in such mundane activities as drawing up an annual budget. In 2010 Sister Jane's budget for Mercy House included a line for "expected donations." As she walked me through the budget for the coming year, I asked how she had determined the figure, which was nearly 4 million UGX (about US$2,000), higher than she had received the year before. She replied, "That number is the difference between what we have and what we need; that's the part we expect that God will provide for us through our friends."

These anticipated gifts were related to the sisters' projected expenditures on "contributions to other causes," listed under "administrative expenses." Surprised to see this item called an administrative expense, I asked Sister Jane why she thought making such donations was an important part of administration. She replied, "We trust in giving that we are able to receive also. As much as we have, we share with others. For example, the other day I put 10,000 UGX (US$5.88) in the collection plate, but I received more. So I believe that when you give, you receive, and not only that, if you want to be helped you should also help others."

Sister Jane was referring to an incident several days earlier when she had taken my husband and me to visit a shrine dedicated to Mary just outside Kampala. The year before I had been searching for an academic job, and unknown to me Sister Jane had stayed awake in the chapel one night praying that I would find one; she had promised God that if her prayer was answered we would visit the shrine. I did indeed find a job, so she insisted we take a day trip there. On the way, she spent 1,000 UGX (US$.60) on a few bottles of water without realizing it was her last small note. During the mass at the shrine, when the collection basket was passed to her, she found only a 10,000 UGX note in her pocket. As the basket passed, I saw her hesitate before giving such a large note. As we were touring the shrine after the mass ended, I asked if we could stop at one of the wholesalers in Kampala on the way back to purchase some school supplies for the children at Mercy House, to thank them for participating in my research. Sister Jane told me about the 10,000 UGX note she had put in the collection basket, interpreting my gift as a divinely sent reciprocation for her offering.

Like prayer, manual labor, and frequent reassignments, such providential practices can thus be seen as a form of ethicomoral equipment. Telling and retelling stories of the "little miracles," laughing aloud in the face of adversity, and formally including gifts from sources yet unknown and contributions to be divinely reciprocated in the annual budget helped the sisters incorporate the discourse of divine Providence into themselves, preparing them to face their struggles with a steadfast commitment to their charism and with faith that God would provide solutions to their problems. Just as the Stoics prepared themselves for misfortune through *praemeditatio malorum* (Foucault 2005, 468–73), so too were the sisters preparing themselves to respond to misfortunes in a way that would confirm, not deny, their love of God.[12]

Proud Beggars

The sisters' faith in divine Providence and their commitment to their charism also altered their relationship with donors and seemed to dispel the fear of losing funding that grips so many in the Ugandan NGO community. In place of this fear there was a powerful trust that they and their charges would be provided for, despite all evidence to the contrary. This trust influenced the sorts of projects the sisters chose to undertake, and it made them less inclined to change their programs to align with trends in the international aid community.

Over the course of my visits, the sisters of Mercy House told and retold the story of the Edmund Mercer Foundation. From my first trip to Mercy House, it was clear that the story of their relationship with the foundation, which I relate below, and the subsequent termination of that relationship was at the center of the sisters' understanding of what their work was about and of their place in the larger philanthropic universe.

One evening Sister Caroline told the story:

In 1983 the late Cardinal Nsubuga, of the Archdiocese of Kampala, got a letter from England concerning that Edmund Mercer man. We had five homes with charity services like this one. . . . The cardinal gave the letter to one of our sisters to go and attend the conference in London concerning this program of Edmund Mercer. It was a good program; they were interested . . . in disability. They said, "You add in the name 'Mercer' and we will do the fundraising." That building [over there] was contributed by that Edmund Mercer man, that small workshop in the middle, the underground water tank, then the Land Rover, the red car, all of that was contributed through [the] Edmund Mercer [Foundation].

During this period the Edmund Mercer Foundation was largely interested in supporting direct care and rehabilitation programs for people with disabilities. Even though working with people with disabilities was only one of the tasks carried out at Mercy House, the staff of the foundation felt that providing direct support for both operational and capital expenses was an effective way of carrying forward this mission, as evinced by the goods and funding the sisters received from the foundation.

Sister Caroline continued, "Edmund Mercer died in 1994. The people who took over after he died, some were carrying on with his vision; others were not. They wanted this home to send away all of the old people and the children [leaving only the disabled]. But caring for those people is part of our charism." The sisters were very angry about the proposed changes and interpreted them as demands that they change their charism to match the desires of a donor: "When Mother Patrick started her ministry, she built the first small thatched hut to look after a boy who wasn't orphaned or disabled, but was simply needy. We could agree to take in more disabled, but we could not get rid of the others." After some time they agreed that they would avoid taking in any more people who fell into the ambiguous "needy" category, limiting future intakes to people with disabilities.

This decision was not without consequences. Sister Caroline continued:

One day an old man came to our gate requesting our help. We turned him away, saying there was nothing we could do given the new policy. The man, dejected, went to the parish priest and told him of the situation. The priest

encouraged him to go back and ask again. But he was so dejected that he refused to come back. Instead we found him hanging from the tree just outside
our compound, having committed suicide. You see, this is the reason we cannot limit our population in the way that another group might.

In mourning, the sisters reflected and prayed and eventually came back
to the position that "it is the charism of the Franciscans to care for the poor
and needy. We ultimately decided to say 'let the money go, let the donors
go,' we will find a way out. We may be beggars, but we are proud beggars."

The sisters felt that making the mission of Mercy House more specific
would require them to change the fundamental mission of their order. Their
ultimate refusal to do this is striking in a climate where NGOs regularly
change their missions, target populations, and approach to match trends in
international funding. Their decision to "let the donors go" placed Mercy
House in a situation of grave financial instability. The statement that "we
will find a way out" reveals their faith in Providence as the force that would
ultimately support them, just as "Disaster," the name of their dog who was
a puppy at the time of the Mercer crisis, reflects their ability to laugh at
their own predicament.

The sisters' faith that God will ultimately provide the means to sustain
their work, which they emphasize by telling and retelling Mother Mary Patrick's own providential encounters with the donor community of her time,
reveals a logic of sustainability, time, and agency that differs from both humanitarianism and development. The sisters of Mercy House believe their
work will be sustained not through their own efforts, but rather through
the work of God and their place in his plan. That they cannot lose their
jobs, which they are committed to for life, reinforces this feeling of stability
and gave them the freedom to say no to the Mercer Foundation. As opposed to NGO workers, whose positions depend on their grants, the sisters'
position is not directly tied to the fate of their funding. Sister Amelia once
assured me that their work would continue whether or not they had donors, since they are obligated to carry it out with or without funds and also
have some assurance of being reassigned by the order should their project
collapse. "We were doing this work before the donors came, and we will
continue doing it even if they leave."

Hope and the Simple Intention

In considering the sisters' faith in Providence and the role Mother Mary
Patrick plays in helping to develop that faith, we begin to understand that

the sisters think about hope, time, grace, and their own agency in the world quite differently from the linear, humanly reachable, midrange future of "developmental time" (Ferguson 1999, 2006). While thinking about this, I came across a copy of Thomas Merton's *No Man Is an Island* (1955) in the sisters' collection of devotional books. In this volume Merton describes the good of working with what he calls "simple intention." He writes, "A simple intention rests in God while accomplishing all things. . . . Since a simple intention does not need to rest in any particular end, it has already reached the end as soon as the work is begun. For the end of a simple intention is to work in God and with Him—to sink deep roots into the soil of His will and to grow there in whatever weather He may bring" (Merton 1955, 62–63).

And so, while the sisters' way of working often struck outsiders who were attached to outcomes as aimless and unpredictable, in looking at Merton's notion that work has "reached the end as soon as the work is begun," we see a pattern in "this jumble of people and needs," which is about more than having too little time and too little money. We move to an understanding of how overcommitted orphanages like Mercy House come to be, when new residents are accepted as having been sent through divine Providence and for the good accomplished in the initial moment of action, with the ultimate results left to God.

Merton's writings reveal how the sisters' ethic of detachment is in many ways at odds with the long-range planning and monitoring that is increasingly required of organizations as they are called on to demonstrate measurable results in order to secure future grants from international organizations. All these measures look to some sort of midrange future, punctuated or otherwise, and seem incompatible with Merton's advocacy for work performed in the present with a simple intention.

By contrast, here we find detachment from the results of work not as a negative, but as something actively promoted. This can be seen in the ways the sisters are regularly moved from one post to another, moves they must accept as part of their vow of obedience. While such transfers proved maddening for some of their donors, the superiors defend them as essential to discourage the sisters from becoming too attached to their projects. Whereas development professionals talk regularly of the need for project "ownership," the sisters were actively discouraged from taking such ownership. This detachment is reflected in their work, for while they are very interested in doing what they do well, they seem markedly less convinced that their actions are the primary cause of whatever results are achieved. Merton's encouragement to work so that one envisions oneself "sink[ing] deep roots into the soil of His will and [growing] there in whatever weather he may bring" (Merton 1955, 62–63) provides a possible explanation for the sisters' resistance to planning and for their relationship to hope and agency.[13]

In his essay on hope as a category of social analysis, Vincent Crapanzano (2003), following Walter Pater, distinguishes the category of hope from the related category of desire, describing hope as desire's "passive counterpart." Hope, he writes, "ultimately . . . depend[s] on the fates—on someone else" (6). Hope's temporal mode, like development's, is linear, teleological, and eschatological; what separates them is the role one's own agency can play in bringing something better into being. Crapanzano's focus on collaborative agency (between God and humans, between the lover and the beloved), on which hope ultimately rests, seems a more accurate description of the role of hope at Mercy House and is reflected in Mother Mary Patrick's reliance on Teresa of Avila's saying, "Teresa and a ducat can do nothing: God, Teresa and a ducat can do everything. Let us do everything we can, but let us make God our banker." In line with this motto, the sisters live in the hope that what they accomplish in the present moment will be perfected and completed by God. This notion of collaborative agency is reflected in their attitude toward the formation process and, as we have seen in this chapter, in the way they approach programmatic decisions at Mercy House. Shaped by an Augustinian anthropology (Lloyd 2008, Brown 1967), they understand themselves as essentially broken and incapable of truly molding themselves to religious life, or accomplishing anything, without God's grace. This same theme is repeated in Catholic theologies of salvation, in which God's will (grace) perfects human action (works). The sisters, like other Catholics, live in the hope that God will make up for their shortcomings, and this faith helps them avoid becoming preoccupied with their own salvation.

This particular historically contingent form of hope (Bloch 1986) can be conceived of as a method, but not quite in the sense in which Ernst Bloch and Hirokazu Miyazaki conceive of it. Bloch and Miyazaki see hope as a philosophical method that focuses not on what is, but on what is "not yet" (Bloch 1986; Miyazaki 2004, 2008). Although the sisters' prayers are at times oriented toward the "not yet," their attitude toward their own role in bringing this "not yet" into being, and the subsequent focus on the importance of living within the eternity of the present moment, makes this formulation an awkward match. For the sisters of Mercy House, hope is not only a philosophical method, but also an end in itself, for it is inextricably tied to both faith and love (1 Cor. 13:13).

Conclusion

Through their activities at Mercy House and the deployment of ethical equipment, the Franciscan Sisters of Africa work to cultivate a sense of accountability to God and a faith in divine Providence. This faith alters their orientation to the future and their belief in their own capacity to influence what that future may hold. By exploring the effects of this particular understanding of time, hope, grace, and human agency, I have shown that otherworldly hopes are not necessarily paralyzing but may enable actions and movement. Yet the ways they do this are often quite different from the stepwise planning associated with political advocacy or development work. Much like the women engaged in the piety movement in Egypt who have voluntarily embraced a form of life that many would describe as highly restrictive (Mahmood 2004), or the forms of judicious opportunism practiced by young women in postcrisis Cameroon (Johnson-Hanks 2005), this case allows us to see a wider range of actions as agentive or intentional.

Using Foucault's writings on ethics, I have explored the forms of ethical work the sisters use to develop this mode of thinking about time and agency, detailing how this ethicotemporal mode separates the interventions the sisters have chosen to undertake from those made by more mainstream development and humanitarian organizations. Not only do the sisters struggle to trust in the divine guidance of their placements (which may put them in situations very different from those they imagined when they entered the novitiate) and to fight the worries that inevitably arise when, for example, the storehouse is nearly empty, but they also struggle to find a way of "living a consecrated life in a rapidly changing world," as the theme of their 2004 chapter meeting phrased it.

In recent years, one of the ways this theme has manifested itself has been through the superiors of the Franciscan Sisters of Africa's enrolling more sisters in business management courses and placing more sisters in apostolates that generate funds to support the order as a whole. To some degree these are pragmatic choices, since the order depends on the salaries earned by sisters assigned to hospitals and schools, where funds are collected through medical bills and school fees, to support its administration, the training of new sisters, and the care of the retired sisters. Yet these choices have also led to tensions between some superiors and those sisters assigned to Mercy House, who see themselves as carrying on the central mission of the order with decreasing support.

Despite these changes, the sisters assigned to work at Mercy House have in many ways remained rooted in the present moment, not conceiving of themselves as "fixing the world" or "solving" anything. This is not "the end of poverty" that Jeffery Sachs promises (Sachs 2005). Instead they see themselves working to better love their neighbor and, through these actions, loving God in a way that focuses simultaneously on the immediate present and on eternity. Where many aid workers see possibilities for better futures brought about through their own planning and agency, the sisters at Mercy House have a far more limited view of their own potency. Although they feel they are working within God's divine plan, they do not see themselves as able to bring about social change without divine intervention. In their embrace of the simple intention, they believe that only God can complete and perfect their imperfect works, which are always broken and always partial, as they believe themselves to be. It is thus that we find that the giver of charity is not the complete human who strategically distributes surplus to the broken poor. In the sisters' understanding, the giver is also broken, and her actions can be completed only through divine grace.

The form of detachment that comes from this way of thinking about agency paradoxically allows these sisters to remain committed to their charism and to forms of social action that are becoming increasingly marginal in international development, including the direct provision of charitable aid.

SEVEN

Conclusion: The Politics and Antipolitics of Charity and Sustainable Development

With this book I have offered a way to think about contemporary development efforts in relation to Kiganda practices of both reciprocal and non-reciprocal caregiving and gift giving. I have argued that while sustainable development programs, such as those run by Hope Child, are hailed internationally as an example of best practice, their avoidance of material "handouts" is understood locally as a failure to recognize the obligations of patronage these organizations have entered into by asking for villagers' labor and contributions. By contrast, redistributive forms of Catholic charity that appear to be both unsustainable and capable of creating dangerous patterns of dependence are locally understood to be complexly intertwined with moral ideals of *mukisa* (kindness), which is proper for reciprocal relations between patron and client, and the Kiganda virtue of *omutima omuyambi* (heart for helping others), which leads one to engage in nonreciprocal gift giving with those in need. My analysis of charity challenges assumptions concerning the ubiquity of obligations of reciprocity and stands in opposition to arguments concerning the unavoidable violence of the charitable gift (Bourdieu 1977, 2000).

In addition to these arguments concerning the morality and "dangers" of various forms of gift giving, this book has explored how organizations oriented toward sustainable development and charity approach questions of accountability, temporality, and their own potency in the world. The sustainable development assemblage is intimately tied to principles of cost-effectiveness and demands that organizations monitor and evaluate their programs in exacting, quantitative terms. Here the highly visible form of a technically correct report is infused with meaning and trust, while the individual actors become relatively interchangeable provided they have the skills needed to create the required documents. This seemingly mundane form of establishing the accountability and effectiveness of an organization is at once part of a process that governs the actions of NGO employees and volunteers and a set of skills that NGO volunteers actively take up to make themselves more employable.

By contrast, charity as practiced at Mercy House relies very little on visible proofs of accountability, depending instead on the trust placed in people shaped through long and ongoing self-cultivation. These techniques not only shape the sisters' approach to accountability, but also influence how they approach time and the limits of their own agency in the world. While their fervent belief in God's involvement in daily affairs could be paralyzing, I argue that it is precisely their sense of living in a world ordered by divine Providence that makes it possible for them to reject the ever-shifting priorities of the international philanthropic community.

This final point brings me to address two overarching questions in this conclusion: What are the political stakes of charity and of sustainable development? And how might you, as a reader, take up the arguments presented as you consider your own engagement with the world?

These overall questions were clarified for me through a number of queries by colleagues who reviewed these chapters. They asked about the political stakes of my arguments, particularly the arguments I make about Mercy House. What is the relation between charity and deeply entrenched poverty? Does a focus on the present with a microscale orientation relinquish social progress, or a better earthly future created through shared struggle?[1] As Farmer (2003) and Rivkin-Fish (2011) ask, Might such charitable activities naturalize poverty and inequality, thus constituting forms of structural violence? Do those engaged in charity have a stake in keeping people in poverty so as to maintain a population to whom they can distribute the alms necessary to achieve their own salvation? In raising these questions, my colleagues were voicing well-justified concerns that development practitioners and other pragmatically minded readers might also want answered. They were asking me to respond to concerns that charity may justify and perpetuate poverty and inequality. They asked if charity and political action can coexist, and if charity transforms only the giver. These are tremendously important questions, and in these last pages I offer some preliminary answers.

The Catholic charity practiced at Mercy House can be seen as in opposition to some forms of political activity. Indeed, as I described in chapter 4, there were some instances when the sisters explicitly contrasted their hands-on approach with political advocacy. While it would be a mistake to draw a hard line between religion and politics or to argue that the sisters oppose an expansion of state-led welfare programs or laws that protect the rights of children or people with disabilities, they do not see political action toward these ends as central to their charism. Instead, they have chosen to stand apart from active engagement in politics. This decision is in part a result of their double marginality, first as members of the Catholic Church (which is a politically marginal institution in Uganda [Gifford 1998]), and second as women within a male-dominated institution. Yet at the same time their lack of involvement in state politics also reflects an active decision to engage with suffering through a different, more present-oriented idiom.

Does this decision to engage in charity in a way that eschews overt political activism have the same depoliticizing effects that have been written about in relation to development and humanitarianism (Fassin 2007; Malkki 1996; Redfield 2012; Rieff 2002; Ticktin 2011)? James Ferguson's *Antipolitics Machine* (1990) set this particular strand of critique in motion by demonstrating how multilateral aid projects depoliticize what are fundamentally political problems while allowing for government expansion in a way that appears technical, not political. This argument has been taken up in many variations since then, and one can argue that one could make similar claims about the work of the nuns at Mercy House. Yet there are aspects of Mercy House and similar charitable institutions that make analyzing it in terms of an antipolitical logic problematic.

Many of the arguments concerning the antipolitics of humanitarianism and development have focused on state or quasi-state actors (Ferguson 1990; Rieff 2002; Ticktin 2011). In these cases humanitarianism is performed as a substitute for more direct political action. For example, Miriam Ticktin describes how the French government applied the illness clause in its immigration law to allow undocumented citizens with diseases untreatable in their home countries to remain in France. This humanitarian gesture served as a substitute for more substantial immigration reforms, and it effectively undermined political movements that demanded greater fundamental changes to state policy (Ticktin 2011). Journalist David Rieff has similarly documented how humanitarian interventions have been used as a cover for a lack of direct military intervention, as in Bosnia in the early 1990s, and as a depoliticized and virtually incontestable rationale for the United States' intervention in Afghanistan at the start of the twenty-first century. In both cases the logic, language, and techniques of humanitarianism served to depoliticize political situations and allowed governments to act or decline to act according to their own interests while avoiding overt political debates (Rieff 2002). Given Mercy House's lack of contact with the Ugandan government, the latter analytic is clearly a poor fit. That said, focusing on alleviating suffering in the immediate present can distract attention from efforts to see and respond to suffering within its larger political and historical context, but I argue that this is a only a possible outcome, not a necessary one.

It might be better to consider Mercy House's refusal to engage in political advocacy as a pragmatic expression of their belief that the present Ugandan government is unlikely to implement reforms that will have any substantial effect on the lives of its people and as a quiet form of political protest. In refusing to act "as if" the Ugandan state were willing or able to undertake substantial reforms, the sisters of Mercy House quietly attest to its weakness. In this light, the advocacy efforts of organizations like the African Center for the Rights of the Child, as decried by Sister Valentine in chapter 4, are far more questionable, given their implicit endorsement of the state's commitment to the lives of its most vulnerable citizens.

The allure of such "as if" engagements with the state was revealed to me during a conference sponsored by the one of Hope Child's funders, centering on early childhood education policy. Over the course of a week, I worked alongside staff members from the Frans Lansing Foundation and their African partner organizations to fill flipchart pages with descriptions of existing policies and lists of the possible roles and responsibilities of various stakeholders.

This particular conference took place in October 2007, just as Zimbabwe was nearing the bottom of its spiral into economic and political crisis. With a 135.62 percent month-after-month inflation rate that reached a mind-boggling 79.6 billion percent by November 2008 and with severe food shortages, many families were finding it impossible to feed their children. Despite these issues, the delegation from Zimbabwe proudly presented their country's early childhood development policy, which was applauded for including two years of compulsory preschool. Privately, members of the Zimbabwe delegation talked about the food shortages and were eager to go shopping in Kampala to stock up on clothes, cell phones, and other goods before heading home. In hallway discussions, the conference participants acknowledged it was unlikely that Zimbabwe's government would allocate resources to accomplish the responsibilities being assigned to it, but this seemed of little concern in the context of exercises whose formal quality abetted the infinite deferral of these issues. The practical requirement that conference participants ignore political realities is perhaps what makes conferences like this so attractive. It allows people to live, even for a moment, in a world where things work as they would like them to. It is easy to pretend that the government will do what it promises in these exercises, and the doubtful nature of this assumption is more or less ignored. The air-conditioned luxury hotel only adds to the effect.

The Franciscan Sisters of Africa's dislike of these "as if" interactions with the government can be seen not only in their critiques of workshops, conferences, and advocacy-based approaches, but also in their response to the more politically engaged efforts of their foreign counterparts. Here I am reminded of a conversation between Sister Caroline and an American nun who had just arrived from the airport on her way to an annual conference for Franciscan priests, nuns, and brothers. The American sister gripped the backseat of the sisters' minibus taxi as it bounced along, her bright blue eyes taking in the view of the road. Her white hair was buzzed into a crew cut, and she wore a T-shirt promoting an antiglobal poverty campaign, reading "Poverty Is the Worst Form of Violence," and a rubber bracelet from Bono's ONE campaign, which asks countries to donate 1 percent of their GDP to foreign aid. After listening politely while Sister Caroline talked about orphanages and hospitals that the Franciscan Sisters of Africa were running, the American nun interjected a question about the effect debt relief had had on the lives of rural Ugandans. "We all worked so hard to campaign for Jubilee 2000,[2] and Uganda is one of the few countries that has seen real debt relief," she said. Sister Caroline laughed, saying, "All the money just stays with the government anyway; I don't think anyone in the villages will ever see that money. Maybe in Mbarara, where the president's people are from, they have seen some of that money. The cows in Mbarara are treated better than our people are here. . . . [President] Museveni does nothing for the poor, and I don't think much can be accomplished by lobbying them." The American sister seemed taken aback by Sister Caroline's lack of hope and her narrow focus on providing direct services to the poor, but after a brief pause she continued discussing her hopes for microfinance and the possibility of establishing a mosquito net factory in Uganda. This conversation speaks not only to Sister Caroline's pragmatic skepticism about collaboration with the Ugandan state, but also to the great variety of approaches to political activism within the Catholic Church.

As this story shows, the Franciscan Sisters of Africa's refusals of more overt political engagement is not a choice forced on them or an act of ignorance, but rather a form of protest. This refusal is not unlike the negative agency Holly Wardlow describes in her writing on passenger women in Papua New Guinea who exchange sex for money outside marriage, thereby reducing the chances that their kin will receive bride price through their marriage. These women are accused of engaging in "a kind of theft [or] the selfish consumption of a resource that rightfully belongs to [their] kin" (Wardlow 2004, 1031). While this may seem a highly unlikely comparison, Wardlow's (2006) insight into the "negative agency" entailed in withholding or refusing to engage speaks to the agency involved in the sisters' refusals to contribute their time and endorsement to workshops and advocacy efforts.[3]

While most of the questions posed to me about the stakes of my argument concerned the political implications of charity, Hope Child's willingness to engage in sustainable development embraces an antipolitics of a different sort. It reinforces the neoliberal proposition that a community can provide its own public goods through voluntary labor and cost-recovery mechanisms such as user fees. This way of thinking about development as a problem to be solved at the village level has been heartily embraced by the Ugandan state, and Hope Child's acceptance of this model seems to me to endanger state-led welfare schemes that might be proposed by those interested in political action more than the charity of Mercy House.

Finally, the arguments Ruth Marshall (2009) and Kevin O'Neill (2010) make in defining a much broader range of actions as "political" in their work on Pentecostals in Nigeria and Guatemala, respectively, raise a series of questions about charity in relation to the established arguments of the antipolitics of development and humanitarianism. If we can accept conversion, prayer, and attempts at self-transformation as forms of political action, then the line between "apolitical" charity and more direct forms of "political" advocacy begins to blur.

Ultimately the sisters' decision to engage in charity in the way they do represents a way of thinking that focuses on what they, as individuals and as a community, ought to do, not on developing a definitive solution to the problem of poverty. Taking a cue from their approach, we find that the normative question to be addressed undergoes an important shift. We move from asking the abstract "How can we bring about the end of poverty?" to the personal "What ethical possibilities are open to me in my particular position?" While resisting the prescriptive impulse this question raises, I close by drawing attention to what the preceding pages tell us about the possible answers to this second question. I take this up with specificities of Uganda in mind because it is always necessary to think about this question in relation to the ethics of those we are engaged with. This allows for multiple ways of imagining what "the good" might be and requires that we look for ways to bring our own understanding of ethics into dialogue with those of others.

In reflecting on this question in relation to Kiganda ethics, I have often thought of the disjuncture between Hope Child's reliance on the image of the interdependent African village and its simultaneous exclusion of itself or its foreign donors from that vision. I think of a walled compound containing Sebanda's residents, who are supposed to work together in harmony and solidarity. This is the proverbial village that is expected to "raise a child." While NGOs and their donors might occasionally enter this walled compound to make a one-time gift or to hold seminars for the people within, they are effectively forbidden to maintain an ongoing material relationship. Although proponents of sustainable development claim the wall exists to protect the villagers from dependence, I argue that donors have built this imaginary wall to protect themselves. If the NGOs and donors were to tear it down, they would have to consider themselves part of that community and thus be subject to the demands of villagers seeking to create deeper social and material relationships. The socially and materially thick relationships that might result would prevent cosmopolitan donors and NGOs from moving easily from place to place and would undoubtedly decrease the number of people they could claim as beneficiaries. But in exchange for their reports and their freedom, they might actually see real improvement in people's lives.

While there are certainly problems with things like child sponsorship programs (Bornstein 2001, 2003), in some ways such programs most closely mimic the types of relationships Ugandans—motivated by ethics of patronage, kinship, and *mutima*—enter into with one another. To enter into such a relationship—even one mediated by a bureaucracy and reliant on problematic images and narratives that exaggerate the isolation of African orphans—is in some ways to position oneself as being inside the wall, as being someone others might attach themselves to. In a different sense we might also consider Partners in Health, a United States–based NGO founded by the medical anthropologist Paul Farmer that provides advanced health care for the poor in countries including Haiti, Peru, Rwanda, and Russia. It has historically worked through a model that attempts to allow its physicians to make the same decisions they would make if they were in a doctor-patient relationship in a hospital in the United States. Partners in Health has made an institutional commitment to act as if it were part of the same world as the people it aims to serve (Farmer 2001). Neither child sponsorships nor Partners in Health will bring about an end to global poverty, but they do represent possible responses to the ethical problem of living in a world shaped by inequality. Yet, as this book had made clear, such approaches are increasingly rare in the contemporary moment, when so many organizations, including those run by the Catholic Church, are focused on a kind of sustainability that encourages them to imagine themselves as separable and separate from those living in the places where they work.

While acknowledging the need for broader forms of political and economic change in Uganda, the limits those making these interventions place on their expectations of what good might arise through their own actions align surprisingly well with contemporary thinking on emergence and the limited good accomplished through purposeful planning. Edward Miguel's hopeful book *Africa's Turn?* points to encouraging signs of economic growth and political progress in Africa but attributes these not to planned development schemes, but to more contingent and unpredictable forces, including rising commodity prices and the growth of China's economy (Miguel 2009). For those who still feel called to act in a world where faith in the power of human planning has largely dissipated, small present-oriented acts of care similar to those made by the sisters seem more promising than the future-oriented vision of sustainable development.

In closing, let me clarify that I am not arguing for a return to charity or other forms of hierarchical giving as universal models for interrelationship. Rather, I believe they should not be rejected out of hand in places where interdependence and hierarchy carry a positive, or at least an ambivalent, moral valence. I hope that by thus unsettling foregone conclusions about the ethics and effects of dependence in the postcolonial world, I have opened a space for reconsidering old and new forms of attachment.

CHAPTER ONE

1. Names of people, places, religious orders, and organizations have been changed to protect the confidentiality of those who participated in the study. Most people in Buganda have two names, one in Luganda chosen from a set of names belonging to their clan and one that is either a Christian or Muslim name. Neither of these are surnames, and either can be used alone. I tried to follow local convention in choosing pseudonyms to allow the texture of naming to come through. In addition, although I have tried to create unique pseudonyms, it is possible that real people, places, and organizations may exist or be created with these names. The only intentional exceptions to this rule are Partners in Health, USAID, Irish Aid, Catholic Relief Services, and the World Food Programme.

2. The Luganda language employs noun classes to denote different categories. In this book I regularly use the prefixes *Ba-, Mu-, Bu-, Lu-,* and *Ki-* to modify the root *-ganda,* so that we have *Baganda* (people belonging to the Baganda ethic group, plural), *Muganda* (a single person belonging to the Baganda ethnic group), *Luganda* (the language spoken by the Baganda), *Buganda* (the place/kingdom where the Baganda live), and *Kiganda* (things and ideas of the Baganda).

3. The rich body of work on personhood among the Tswana of southern Africa is instructive for its descriptions of how building oneself up through relationships speaks to the actions and agency of individuals (Comaroff and Comaroff 2001; Livingston 2005; Klaits 2010).

4. Deborah Durham's (1995) writings on Botswana similarly test the presumption that actors are unencumbered equals before the exchange and that all gifts are made with the expectation of reciprocity.

5. Symbolic violence is a form of coercion that relies on the consent of the dominated. To give this consent, those dominated must understand the situation using concepts and modes of reasoning they share with their dominators (Bourdieu 2000).

6. For a similar discussion of the problem of assuming reciprocity in relation to the practice of *dan* in Hinduism, see Parry (1986) and Bornstein (2012).

7. Anthropologists studying ethics have noted that the lack of sustained inquiry and debate on ethics has resulted in the inconsistent and confusing use of the terms "ethics" and "morality" (Kleinman 1999; Laidlaw 2002; Zigon 2008). For example, Arthur Kleinman's attempt to distinguish ethics and morality is deeply informed

by his interest in the relation between the use of principalism in biomedical ethics and the complex ethicomoral quandaries of medical practice. This focus led him to define ethics as a set of formal abstract rules or principles and morality as the messy enactment of these rules in daily life. Using this definition draws attention to the need for anthropology as a method for elucidating the details of moral experience, in contrast to the study of formal ethical systems (Kleinman 1999). Yet, while his definitions make sense in the context of biomedicine, they are quite different from those developed by other anthropologists and philosophers studying ethics and morality. James Laidlaw's definition of ethics is closer to the Aristotelian sense in that it focuses on *phronêsis*, the practical ability to make judgments about right action in specific situations. Following this tradition, Laidlaw defines ethics as a situation-dependent practice informed by self-training. This definition of ethics is anything but the application of a system of formal rules (Laidlaw 2002). This definition also seems to see all ethical systems in terms of virtue ethics. Following Nietzsche, Laidlaw uses the term "morality" in a more limited sense to refer to a subset of ethical systems where "self-denying values inform law-like obligations" (317). More recently, Jarrett Zigon has attempted to distinguish ethics, which he defines as those moments in which troubled actors consciously reflect on their actions and work on themselves, from morality, which he defines as the embodied and largely untroubled enactment of the good in daily life that is informed by institutions and public discourse (Zigon 2008, 180). In this book I have decided to forestall resolution of this debate and use the terms "ethics," "morals," and "ethicomoral" interchangeably to refer to assemblages of technologies, norms, practices, and modes of reasoning related to situated judgment about "the right" or "the good."

8. For an excellent discussion of ethicomoral transformation, see Robbins (2004).

9. In 2007–8, southern Uganda's peace contrasted with northern Uganda, where a brutal war between the Lord's Resistance Army and the Ugandan government had been raging since 1986. See Finnström (2008) for an excellent account of the war and its impact on the Acholi people.

10. After the decline and discrediting of charity in the eighteenth century (see chapter 2), philanthropy reemerged in the nineteenth century with a focus on the child. Relying on the emergent ideas of natural rights, the existence of "childhood" as a period of innocence and dependence deserving special protection, and the importance of forming children as protocitizens, the child emerged as a figure who might appropriately depend on adults and institutions apart from the family of origin. For an overview of this history, see Cunningham (1995).

11. Catholic Relief Services is the official international humanitarian and development organization of the Catholic community of the United States of America. It is not affiliated with Mercy House.

12. See Ado Tiberondwa (1998) on the ways the mission-led educational experiences of local leaders were central to the economic, political, and cultural exploitation of the Ugandan people under colonial rule.

13. Although there have been a number of ethnographic studies of Catholicism, they have been fewer and less widely circulated than those on Pentecostalism. (See, for example, Cannell 1999; Green 2003; Simpson 2003a, 2003b; Orta 2004; Lester 2005; Vokes 2005; Wiegele 2005; Mayblin 2010, 2012; and Behrend 2011.)

14. The Catholic Charismatic Renewal is a movement within the Catholic Church that began in the 1960s. It emphasizes the gifts of the Holy Spirit and often involves

prayer meetings during which people are encouraged to connect directly with God through song, prayer, speaking in tongues, and faith healing.

CHAPTER TWO

1. Before the second millennium, the Baganda used an agricultural system based on tubers, beans, sorghum, and finger millet grown in fields that could be worked for only a few years at a time. Soil erosion, decreased rainfall, and overcultivation between 950 and 1100 may have created land shortages that made the shift to banana cultivation an attractive innovation (Hanson 2003).

2. Mailo land is land allocated by square miles (640 acres) and controlled as private property.

3. Limits on the access to high-quality schooling, particularly secondary and tertiary education, began to change in the later decades of the colonial period when both government and missionary organizations created scholarships to finance the education of children from poor backgrounds.

4. For a discussion of *mutima* as the seat of thought, wisdom, and memory, see Orley (1970).

5. See, for example, discussions of the inculcation of *mpisa* (culture, custom, conduct) in children (Kilbride and Kilbride 1990, 89; Cheney 2007, 59; Karlström 2004).

6. This concept of tithing as a form of redistributive justice was taken up in the Christian tradition in the writings of the sixth-century Pope Gregory, who wrote, "For when we minister what is necessary to the indigent we bestow not what is ours, but what rightly belongs to them. In fact, we pay a debt of justice, not an act of mercy" (Gregory 2007, 146).

7. A papal encyclical is a letter or essay written by the pope to all the bishops. These encyclicals are meant to instruct the clergy and laity on the current teachings of the Catholic Church.

8. John Hanning Speke and James Augustus Grant first introduced Christianity in Uganda in 1862. In 1875, Kabaka Mutesa I, himself a convert to Islam, felt that an alliance with the British might be helpful and asked his chiefs to choose between the Quran and the Bible. The chiefs allegedly chose the Bible, and Henry Morgan Stanley hired a freed Malawian slave, who himself never converted, to translate an abridged version of the Bible and the Gospel of Luke into Luganda (Baur 2001).

9. I have found it necessary to use the pseudonyms Mother Mary Patrick and the Franciscan Sisters of Africa to protect the confidentiality of the sisters and residents of Mercy House.

10. For an excellent history of participatory development, see Green (2000).

11. For an extended discussion of this project, see Li (2007).

CHAPTER THREE

1. I use George Mpanga's real name with his permission and in recognition of his contributions to this project.

2. The exchange rate during my fieldwork in 2007–8 was approximately 1,700 UGX to US$1. Based on that exchange rate, the average annual per capita income in Uganda was approximately 510,000 UGX (US$300), and a casual laborer in Sebanda was paid 1,000 UGX to 5,000 UGX (US$.60 to $2.94) for a day's work.

3. This argument builds on the writings of other scholars who have argued that, despite their populist appearance, participatory approaches to sustainable development

often fail to match local expectations concerning the various exchanges involved (Green and Chambers 2006; West 2006; Li 2007; Swidler and Watkins 2009). Several scholars have also challenged the long-term sustainability of these so-called cost-effective sustainable projects (Kremer and Miguel 2007). Others have argued that sustainable development practices such as microfinance and user fees have decreased the focus on the poor (Morduch 1999); diminished household prosperity and food consumption (Brett 2006); and created precipitous declines in health care utilization (Meuwissen 2002). Paul Farmer (2003) has criticized the way sustainability and cost-effectiveness have been used to argue for a sort of "managed inequality" and substandard care for the poor. Others have mounted critiques of projects that purport to be participatory yet continue to implement agendas set by donor interests and to favor the interests of elite community members at the expense of others, except when they need their consent and labor (Rahnema 1992; Cooke and Kothari 2001; High 2009). Yet despite these critiques, sustainable participatory development has retained its prominent position within development discourse and practice.

4. In Uganda, *matatu* (taxi) refers to large white vans that seat fourteen. These taxis regularly travel along most major roads.

5. *Matooke* is the Luganda word for a cooking banana, a traditional staple of the Baganda diet.

6. *Boda-bodas* are motorcycle or bicycle taxis that carry one or two passengers on a seat directly behind the driver.

7. A borehole is a water well with a hand pump.

8. For a related critique of the use of rights discourse in Malawi, see Englund (2006).

9. David Mosse (2004), Kathleen O'Reilly (2010) and Maxine Weisgrau (1997) have noted similar linkages between participation and patronage in South Asia, where NGO workers are sometimes able to provide the expected access to government subsidies and other material benefits. Dan Smith (2004) and Ann Swidler and Susan C. Watkins (2007) have also described how NGOs allow their employees to act as patrons who compete for clients in the form of NGO volunteers through the distribution of transport per diems. NGO volunteers, in turn, support their NGO employer-cum-patron by demonstrating their support for the project during monitoring visits from international donors.

10. On the selection of elite beneficiaries, see Abramson (1999).

11. For the symbolic importance of collecting and documenting information in the context of clinical trials, see Heimer (2012).

CHAPTER FOUR

1. The term "charism" in this context refers to the beliefs, commitments, and mission of a particular order.

2. Although my analysis focuses on patronage and *omutima omuyambi* as they have emerged in Buganda, many of the sisters were members of other ethnic groups in Uganda, Kenya, and Tanzania. The presence of people from multiple ethnic groups has the potential to complicate matters, but I saw no major differences in how people conceptualized ethical dilemmas, which could be easily traced along lines of ethnicity.

3. Kwashiorkor is a form of malnutrition caused by diets extremely low in protein.

4. Related controversies have been at the center of Franciscan debate since the thir-

teenth century. For further reading on these debates in a historical context, see Moorman (1968).

5. Erica Bornstein (2009, 2012) describes a similar tension between the merits of impulsive giving in Hinduism and increasing demands that gifts be sustainable and effective.

6. For a discussion of sacralized solicitory exchanges (gifts made to solicit a counter-gift) among Christians in Papua New Guinea, see Stewart and Strathern (2001).

7. For a similar discussion of vertical chains of support among Zambian Pentecostals, see Haynes (2012b, 136).

8. CHOGM was the Commonwealth Heads of Government Meeting, held in Uganda in 2007.

CHAPTER FIVE

1. For a history of the rise of efficiency as a positive value for both machines and humans, see Alexander (2008).

2. See http://www.genevaglobal.com, accessed March 27, 2013.

3. Others have similarly noted the appeal of low-cost training and workshops as a means of demonstrating quantifiable outputs (Gupta and Sharma 2006; Nguyen 2010).

4. For a nuanced discussion of the aesthetics of NGO documents, see Riles (1998, 2000).

CHAPTER SIX

1. The morning office is one of six sets of prayers and readings that make up the Liturgy of the Hours, which is said throughout the day by the sisters as it is by the monks, nuns, and priests in many religious orders. The prayers and readings follow a regular rotation according to the church calendar. The morning office starts just before dawn and is followed by a mass said by the sisters' chaplain. The evening office is followed by meditation and adoration of the Eucharist.

2. Anthropologists inspired by Foucault's work on ethics have explored how people shape themselves into particular kinds of subjects. Rebecca Lester's ethnography of postulants in a Mexican convent beautifully articulates the role of embodied experience in these processes, describing how the postulants learn to read their bodies "as a sort of barometer" that measures the correspondence between their worldly "experiential self" and their transcendent "virtual self" (Lester 2003). Saba Mahmood's work on women's participation in the Islamic Revival movement in Egypt highlights the distinction between agency and resistance and helps us understand how people actively engage in self-discipline (Mahmood 2004). In addressing the ways that the Franciscan Sisters of Africa think about their own ethical practices, Foucault's model becomes a critical tool, not because it works as a general theory of the ethical that would be applicable in all cases, but because their own model of ethical formation is an extension of monastic practices, which developed out of Greek forms of caring for the self (Foucault 2005).

3. To a certain degree the sisters at Mercy House are also interested in changing the ethicomoral and religious possibilities of those they come in contact with. This is perhaps most explicit in their schools. This said, with the exception of sisters like Sister Christine Namusoke, who continued to work as a catechist in an area with a relatively small Christian population, the sisters live and work in a world where

religion appears as something of a constant. Although the sisters take great pride in the children who have gone on to be active in the church as clergy or laity or who have a special devotion to God, these outcomes are not the accomplishment of an explicit aim. Rather, their work—their own effort to imitate Christ—is for them an end in itself and distinct from evangelizing. This approach contrasts with that of the American evangelicals Omri Elisha describes in his writings on the "compassion fatigue" that faith-based activists experience when the objects of their charity fail to change their behavior (Elisha 2008).

4. Francis of Assisi (1181–1226) founded the Franciscan order—the Friars Minor—in the early thirteenth century after giving up the lifestyle he had enjoyed as the son of a wealthy Umbrian cloth merchant. Saint Clare's request to follow a similar life in 1211 prompted him to found the order of Poor Ladies, a contemplative order now called the Poor Clares. Francis was also involved in founding a third order of lay confraternities and religious institutes that follow similar rules based on poverty, obedience, and chastity while taking up a more active role in the world.

5. For a contrasting description of the pleasures to be found in processes of ethical formation in the Hunza Valley of Pakistan, see Miller (2013).

6. I thank Nina Liss-Schultz for her thoughts on discomfort and ethical practice.

7. A *gomesa* is a long dress with a square neckline and peaked sleeves fastened by a wide belt tied in the front, typically worn in the central region of Uganda. Today it is most often worn by older women or for formal occasions.

8. *Kitengi* refers to the printed cloth commonly seen across much of Africa. While *kitengi* may be worn as a simple wrap skirt, it can also be used in elaborately tailored dresses, skirts, blouses, and head wraps.

9. These internal arguments concerning barriers to possible corruption that are put in place through the vows of poverty, obedience, and chastity are not unlike those made by castrated Hijra politicians claiming incorruptibility (Cohen 1995).

10. *Butaka* is an ancestral burial ground or land belonging to one of Buganda's forty clans.

11. While in some ways an act of resistance against the demands of international donors, the sisters' laughter is different from that described by Achille Mbembe, for whom humorous distortions are of signs of power, which are themselves already part of a shared aesthetics of vulgarity and which allow the postcolonial subject to simultaneously reaffirm and subvert commandment (Mbembe 2001). The sisters' laughter is less an act of subversion than a technique for diminishing the importance of a crisis, for themselves and for others, so as to achieve confidence that the present crisis is somehow part of a divinely ordered plan.

12. There is clearly tension between intensive efforts to shape the self and faith in divine Providence. Stoic (Long 1974; Lloyd 2008) and Christian (Mahoney 1987; McBrien 1994; Lloyd 2008; Brown 1967; Weber 2002) scholars have spent millennia attempting to resolve the apparent contradictions between their belief in a divinely ordered world and their belief that humans must work hard to avoid evil and to align themselves with this divine order. Given that this is one of the most important and philosophically complex tensions within these traditions, it is beyond the scope of this book to summarize or resolve it.

13. Similar perspectives on the present moment can be found in the writings of Simone Weil (1973).

CHAPTER SEVEN

1. I thank an anonymous reviewer for posing this question.
2. Jubilee 2000 was a broad-based interfaith campaign advocating the cancellation of debts owed by deeply indebted poor countries.
3. I want to express special thanks to Betsey Brada for calling my attention to this unexpected comparative case.

REFERENCES

Abramson, David. 1999. "A Critical Look at NGOs and Civil Society as a Means to an End in Uzbekistan." *Human Organization: Journal of the Society for Applied Anthropology* 58: 240–50.

Adams, Bill. 1990. *Green Development: Environment and Sustainability in the Third World.* London: Routledge.

Alexander, Jennifer Karns. 2008. *The Mantra of Efficiency: From Waterwheel to Social Control.* Baltimore: Johns Hopkins University Press.

Anderson, Gary A. 2009. *Faith and Finance: First Things.* http://www.firstthings.com/article/2009/05/faith--finance-1243315689.

Arendt, Hannah. 1958. *The Human Condition.* Chicago: University of Chicago Press.

Baker, Susan. 2006. *Sustainable Development.* London: Routledge.

Baur, John. 2001. *2000 Years of Christianity in Africa.* Nairobi: Paulines Publications Africa.

Bayart, Jean-François. 1989. *The State in Africa: The Politics of the Belly.* London: Longman Press.

Behrend, Heike. 2011. *Resurrecting Cannibals: The Catholic Church, Witch-Hunts, and the Production of Pagans in Western Uganda.* New York: James Currey.

Beidelman, Thomas O. 1986. *Moral Imagination in Kaguru Modes of Thought.* Bloomington: Indiana University Press.

Berg, Elliot. 1982. Accelerated Development in Sub-Saharan Africa: An Agenda for Action. Washington, DC: World Bank.

Bevans, Stephen, and Roger Schroeder. 2004. *Constants in Context: A Theology of Mission for Today.* Maryknoll, NY: Orbis Books.

Bialecki, John, Naomi Haynes, and Joel Robbins. 2008. "The Anthropology of Christianity." *Religion Compass* 2 (6): 1139–58.

Blau, Peter Michael. 1964. *Exchange and Power in Social Life.* New York: John Wiley.

Bloch, Ernst. 1986. *The Principle of Hope.* Cambridge, MA: MIT Press.

Bornstein, Erica. 2001. "Child Sponsorship, Evangelism, and Belonging in the Work of World Vision Zimbabwe." *American Ethnologist* 28 (3): 595–622.

———. 2003. *The Spirit of Development: Protestant NGOs, Morality, and Economics in Zimbabwe.* New York: Routledge.

———. 2009. "The Impulse of Philanthropy." *Cultural Anthropology* 24 (4): 622–51.

———. 2012. *Disquieting Gifts: Humanitarianism in New Delhi.* Stanford, CA: Stanford University Press.

Bornstein, Erica, and Peter Redfield. 2011. *Forces of Compassion: Humanitarianism between Ethics and Politics.* Santa Fe, NM: School for Advanced Research Press.

Bornstein, Lisa, Tina Wallace, and Jennifer Chapman. 2006. *The Aid Chain: Coercion and Commitment in Development NGOs.* Warwickshire, UK: Intermediate Technology.

Bourdieu, Pierre. 1977. *Outline of a Theory of Practice.* Cambridge: Cambridge University Press.

———. 2000. *Pascalian Meditations.* Stanford, CA: Stanford University Press.

Brada, Betsey. 2011. "Botswana as a Living Experiment." PhD diss., University of Chicago.

Brett, Johnathan. 2006. "'We Sacrifice and Eat Less': The Structural Complexities of Microfinance Participation." *Human Organization: Journal of the Society for Applied Anthropology* 65 (1): 8–19.

Brown, Michael. 2010. "A Tale of Three Buildings: Certifying Virtue in the New Moral Economy." *American Ethnologist* 37 (4): 741–52.

Brown, Peter Robert Lamont. 1967. *Augustine of Hippo.* Berkeley: University of California Press.

———. 2002. *Poverty and Leadership in the Later Roman Empire.* Waltham, MA: Brandeis University Press.

Butt, Leslie. 2002. "The Suffering Stranger: Medical Anthropology and International Morality." *Medical Anthropology Quarterly* 21: 1–24.

Calhoun, Craig. 2010. "The Idea of Emergency: Humanitarian Action and Global (Dis) order." In *Contemporary States of Emergency: The Politics of Military and Humanitarian Interventions,* edited by Didier Fassin and Mariella Pandolfi, 29–58. Cambridge, MA: Zone Books.

Cannell, Fenella. 1999. *Power and Intimacy in the Christian Philippines.* New York: Cambridge University Press.

Cardoso, Fernando Henrique, and Enzo Faletto. 1979. *Dependency and Development in Latin America.* Berkeley: University of California Press.

Catholic Church. 1939. *Rerum Novarum.* New York: Paulist Press.

Chabal, Patrick, and Jean-Pascal Daloz. 1999. *Africa Works: Disorder as Political Instrument.* London: International African Institute.

Chambers, Robert. 1983. *Rural Development: Putting the Last First.* New York: Longman.

Cheney, Kristen. 2007. *Pillars of the Nation: Child Citizens and Ugandan National Development.* Chicago: University of Chicago Press.

Cohen, Lawrence. 1995. "The Pleasures of Castration: The Postoperative Status of Hijras, Jankhas and Academics." In *Sexual Nature, Sexual Culture,* edited by Paul R. Abramson and Steven D. Pinkerton, 276–304. Chicago: University of Chicago Press.

Cole, Jennifer. 2010. *Sex and Salvation: Imagining the Future in Madagascar.* Chicago: University of Chicago Press.

Coleman, Simon. 2000. *The Globalisation of Charismatic Christianity: Spreading the Gospel of Prosperity.* Cambridge: Cambridge University Press.

Comaroff, Jean, and John Comaroff. 1991. *On Revelation and Revolution: Christianity, Colonialism, and Consciousness in South Africa,* vol. 1. Chicago: University of Chicago Press.

———. 2001. "On Personhood: An Anthropological Perspective from Africa." *Social Identities* 7 (2): 267–83.

Cooke, Bill, and Uma Kothari. 2001. *Participation: The New Tyranny?* London: Zed Books.

Crapanzano, Vincent. 2003. "Reflections on Hope as a Category of Social and Psychological Analysis." *Cultural Anthropology* 18 (1): 3–32.

Cruikshank, Barbara. 1999. *The Will to Empower: Democratic Citizens and Other Subjects.* Ithaca, NY: Cornell University Press.

Cunningham, Hugh. 1995. *Children and Childhood in Western Society since 1500.* London: Longman.

Dahl, Bianca. 2009. "Left Behind? Orphaned Children, Humanitarian Aid, and the Politics of Kinship, Culture, and Caregiving during Botswana's AIDS Crisis." PhD diss., Univerity of Chicago.

Dean, Mitchell. 1999. *Governmentality: Power and Rule in Modern Society.* London: Sage.

Deleuze, Gilles, and Félix Guattari. 1987. *A Thousand Plateaus: Capitalism and Schizophrenia.* Minneapolis: University of Minnesota Press.

Dicklitch, Susan. 1998. *The Elusive Promise of NGOs in Africa: Lessons from Uganda.* New York: St. Martin's Press.

Douglas, Mary. 1990. "Foreword: No Free Gifts." In *The Gift: Form and Reason from Exchange in Archaic Societies,* edited by Marcel Mauss, vii–xviii. London: Routledge.

Durham, Deborah. 1995. "Soliciting Gifts and Negotiating Agency: The Spirit of Asking in Botswana." *Journal of the Royal Anthropological Institute* 1 (1): 111–28.

Elisha, Omri. 2008. *Moral Ambition: Mobilization and Social Outreach in Evangelical Megachurches.* Berkeley: University of California Press.

Elliott, Jennifer A. 1999. *An Introduction to Sustainable Development.* 2nd ed. New York: Routledge.

Elyachar, Julia. 2005. *Markets of Dispossession: NGOs, Economic Development, and the State in Cairo.* Durham, NC: Duke University Press.

Englund, Harri. 2006. *Prisoners of Freedom: Human Rights and the African Poor.* Berkeley: University of California Press.

Epstein, Helen. 2007. *The Invisible Cure: Africa, the West, and the Fight against AIDS.* New York: Farrar, Straus and Giroux.

Escobar, Arturo. 1995. *Encountering Development.* Princeton, NJ: Princeton University Press.

Fallers, Lloyd. 1964. *The King's Men: Leadership and Status in Buganda on the Eve of Independence.* London: Oxford University Press.

Farmer, Paul. 2001. *Infections and Inequalities: The Modern Plagues.* Berkeley: University of California Press.

———. 2003. *Pathologies of Power: Health, Human Rights, and the New War on the Poor,* vol. 4. Berkeley: University of California Press.

Fassin, Didier. 2007. "Humanitarianism as a Politics of Life." *Public Culture* 19 (3): 499–520.

Ferguson, James. 1990. *The Anti-politics Machine.* Cambridge: Cambridge University Press.

———. 1999. *Expectations of Modernity: Myths and Meanings of Urban Life on the Zambian Copperbelt.* Berkeley: University of California Press.

———. 2006. *Global Shadows: Africa in the Neoliberal World Order.* Durham, NC: Duke University Press.

———. 2013. "Declarations of Dependence: Labor, Personhood, and Welfare in South Africa." *Journal of the Royal Anthropological Institute* 19: 223–42.

Fernando, Jude. 2003. *The Power of Unsustainable Development: What Is to Be Done?* Annals of the American Academy of Political and Social Science, vol. 554, Thousand Oaks, CA: Sage.

Ferris, Elizabeth. 2005. "Faith-Based and Secular Humanitarian Organizations." *International Review of the Red Cross* 87 (858): 311–25.

Finnström, Sverker. 2008. *Living with Bad Surroundings: War, History, and Everyday Moments in Northern Uganda.* Durham, NC: Duke University Press.

Firth, Raymond. 1967. *Themes in Economic Anthropology*, vol. 6. London: Tavistock.

Fisher, William F. 1997. "Doing Good? The Politics and Antipolitics of NGO Practices." *Annual Review of Anthropology* 26: 439–64.

Foucault, Michel. (1977) 1980. "The Confession of the Flesh." In *Power/Knowledge: Selected Interviews and Other Writings 1972–1977*, edited by Colin Gordon, 194–228. New York: Pantheon Books.

———. 1978. *Discipline and Punish: The Birth of the Prison.* Translated by Alan Sheridan. New York: Pantheon Books.

———. 1984. "Nietzsche, Genealology, History." In *The Foucault Reader*, edited by Paul Rabinow, 76–100. New York: Pantheon Books.

———. 1990a. *The History of Sexuality*. Vol. 1, *An Introduction*. New York: Vintage Books.

———. 1990b. *The History of Sexuality*. Vol. 2, *The Use of Pleasure*. New York: Vintage Books.

———. 1997. *Ethics: Subjectivity and Truth.* Edited by Paul Rabinow. Vol. 1 of the *Essential Works of Michel Foucault.* New York: New Press.

———. 2005. *Hermeneutics of the Subject: Lectures at the Collège de France, 1974–1975.* Translated by Graham Burchell, edited by Arnold Davidson. New York: Palgrave Macmillian.

———. 2007. *Security, Territory, Population: Lectures at the Collège de France, 1977–78.* Translated by Graham Burchell, edited by Arnold Davidson. New York: Palgrave Macmillan.

———. 2008. *The Birth of Biopolitics: Lectures at the Collège de France, 1978–79.* Translated by Graham Burchell, edited by Arnold Davidson. New York: Palgrave Macmillan.

Frank, Andre Gunder. 1967. *Capitalism and Underdevelopment in Latin America: Historical Studies of Chile and Brazil.* New York: Monthly Review Press.

Gale, Hubert P. 1959. *Uganda and the Mill Hill Fathers.* London: Macmillan.

Gifford, Paul. 1998. *African Christianity: Its Public Role.* Bloomington: Indiana University Press.

Godelier, Maurice. 1999. *The Enigma of the Gift.* Chicago: University of Chicago Press.

Green, Jessica F., and William Bradnee Chambers. 2006. *The Politics of Participation in Sustainable Development Governance.* New York: United Nations University Presss.

Green, Maia. 2000. "Participatory Development and the Appropriation of Agency in Southern Tanzania." *Critique of Anthropology* 20 (1): 67–89.

———. 2003. *Priests, Witches and Power: Popular Christianity after Mission in Southern Tanzania.* Cambridge: Cambridge University Press.

Gregory. 2007. *The Book of Pastoral Rule.* Translated by George E. Demacopoulos. Crestwood, NY: Saint Vladimir's Seminary Press.

Gupta, Akhil. 2012. *Red Tape: Bureaucracy, Structural Violence, and Poverty in India.* Durham, NC: Duke University Press.

Gupta, Akhil, and Aradhana Sharma. 2006. "Globalization and Postcolonial States." *Current Anthropology* 47 (2): 277–307.

Guyer, Jane. 2007. "Prophecy and the Near Future: Thoughts on Macroeconomic, Evangelical, and Punctuated Time." *American Ethnologist* 34 (3): 409–21.

Guyer, Jane, and Samuel M. Eno Belinga. 1995. "Wealth in People as Wealth in Knowledge: Accumulation and Composition in Equatorial Africa." *Journal of African History* 36: 91–120.

Hackett, Roslind. 1995. "The Gospel of Prosperity in West Africa." In *Religion and the Transformations of Capitalism: Comparative Approaches*, edited by R. H. Roberts, 199–214. London: Routledge.

Halvorson, Britt. 2012. "Woven Worlds: Material Things, Bureaucratization, and Dilemmas of Caregiving in Lutheran Humanitarianism." *American Ethnologist* 39 (1) 122–37.

Hanson, Holly Elisabeth. 2003. *Landed Obligation: The Practice of Power in Buganda*. Portsmouth, NH: Heinemann.

Harding, Susan Friend. 2000. *The Book of Jerry Falwell: Fundamentalist Language and Politics*. Princeton, NJ: Princeton University Press.

Hastings, Adrian. 1995. *The Church in Africa, 1450–1950*. Oxford: Clarendon Press.

Haynes, Naomi. 2012a. "Ambitious Obligations: Pentecostalism, Social Life, and Political Economy on the Zambian Copperbelt." PhD diss., University of California, San Diego.

———. 2012b. "Pentecostalism and the Morality of Money: Prosperity, Inequality, and Religious Sociality on the Zambian Copperbelt." *Journal of the Royal Anthropological Institute* 18 (1): 123–39.

Heimer, Carol. 2008. "Thinking about How to Avoid Thought: Deep Norms, Shallow Rules, and the Structure of Attention." *Regulation and Governance* 2: 30–47.

———. 2012. "Inert Facts and the Illusion of Knowledge: Strategic Uses of Ignorance in HIV Clinics." *Economy and Society* 41 (1): 17–41.

Herzfeld, Michael. 1992. *The Social Production of Indifference: Exploring the Symbolic Roots of Western Bureaucracy*. Chicago: University of Chicago Press.

High, Holly. 2009. "The Road to Nowhere? Poverty and Policy in the South of Laos." *Focaal*, no. 53: 75–88.

Hindness, Barry. 2004. "Liberalism—What's in a Name?" In *Global Governmentality: Governing International Spaces*, edited by W. Larner and W. Walters, 23–39. London: Routledge.

Hobsbawm, Eric, and Terence Ranger. 1982. *The Invention of Tradition*. Cambridge: Cambridge University Press.

Homberg, Johan, and Richard Sandbrook. 1992. "Sustainable Development: What Is to Be Done?" In *Policies for a Small Planet*, edited by Johan Holmberg, 19–38. London: Earthscan.

Hunter, Susan S. 2003. *Black Death: AIDS in Africa*. New York: Palgrave Macmillan.

Iliffe, John. 1979. *A Modern History of Tanganyika*. Cambridge: Cambridge University Press.

Johnson-Hanks, Jennifer. 2005. "When the Future Decides: Uncertainty and Intentional Action in Contemporary Cameroon." *Current Anthropology* 46 (3): 363–85.

Jones, Colin. 1982. *Charity and Bienfaisance: The Treatment of the Poor in the Montpellier Region, 1740–1815*. Cambridge: Cambridge University Press.

Karlström, Mikael. 2004. "Modernity and Its Aspirants: Moral Community and Developmental Eutopianism in Buganda." *Current Anthropology* 45 (5): 595–619.

Kilbride, Philip Leroy, and Janet Capriotti Kilbride. 1990. *Changing Family Life in East Africa: Women and Children at Risk*. University Park: Pennsylvania State University Press.

Kiwanuka, M. S. M. Semakula. 1972. *A History of Buganda from the Foundation of the Kingdom to 1900*. New York: Africana.

Klaits, Fred. 2010. *Death in a Church of Life: Moral Passion during Botswana's Time of AIDS*. Berkeley: University of California Press.

———. 2011. "Asking as Giving: Apostolic Prayers and the Aesthetics of Well-Being in Botswana." *Journal of Religion in Africa* 41 (2): 206–26.

Kleinman, Arthur. 1999. "Moral Experience and Ethical Reflection: Can Ethnography Reconcile Them? A Quandary for "the New Bioethics." *Daedalus* 128 (4): 69–97.

Kollman, Paul V. 2005. *The Evangelization of Slaves and Catholic Origins in Eastern Africa.* Maryknoll, NY: Orbis Books.

Kopytoff, Igor, and Suzanne Miers. 1977. *Slavery in Africa: Historical and Anthropological Perspectives.* Madison: University of Wisconsin Press.

Kremer, Michael, and Edward Miguel. 2007. "The Illusion of Sustainability." *Quarterly Journal of Economics* 122 (3): 1007–65.

Laidlaw, James. 2002. "For an Anthropology of Ethics and Freedom." *Journal of the Royal Anthropological Institute* 8 (2): 311–32.

Lester, Rebecca J. 2003. "The Immediacy of Eternity: Time and Transformation in a Roman Catholic Convent." *Religion* 33 (3): 201–19.

———. 2005. *Jesus in Our Wombs: Embodying Modernity in a Mexican Convent,* vol. 5. Berkeley: University of California Press.

Letts, Christine, William Ryan, and Allen Grossman. 1997. "Virtuous Capital: What Foundations Can Learn from Venture Capitalists." *Harvard Business Review,* March-April, 36–39 and 41–44.

Leve, Lauren G. 2001. "Between Jesse Helms and Ram Bahadur: Participation and Empowerment in Women's Literacy Programming in Nepal." *PoLAR: Political and Legal Anthropology Review* 24 (1): 108–28.

Li, Tania Murray. 2007. *The Will to Improve: Governmentality, Development, and the Practice of Politics.* Durham, NC: Duke University Press.

Livingston, Julie. 2005. *Debility and the Moral Imagination in Botswana.* Bloomington: Indiana University Press.

Lloyd, Genevieve. 2008. *Providence Lost.* Cambridge, MA: Harvard University Press.

Long, A. A. 2001. *Hellenistic Philosphy: Stoics, Epircureans, Sceptics.* London: Duckworth.

Louis, Mary. 1964. *Love Is the Answer: The Story of Mother [Patrick].* Dublin: Fallon's Educational Supply. (The name has been changed to preserve the anonymity of Mercy House.)

Low, Donald Anthony. 1971a. *Buganda in Modern History.* London: Weidenfeld and Nicolson.

———. 1971b. *The Mind of Buganda: Documents of the Modern History of an African Kingdom.* Berkeley: University of California Press.

Luhrmann, Tanya Marie. 2012. *When God Talks Back: Understanding the American Evangelical Relationship with God.* New York: Alfred A. Knopf.

Mahmood, Saba. 2004. *Politics of Piety: The Islamic Revival and the Feminist Subject.* Princeton, NJ: Princeton University Press.

Mahoney, John. 1987. *The Making of Moral Theology: A Study of the Roman Catholic Tradition.* London: Clarendon Press.

Malkki, Liisa. 1996. "Speechless Emissaries: Refugees, Humanitarianism, and Dehistorization." *Cultural Anthropology* 11 (3): 377–404.

Mallaby, Sebastian. 2004. *The World's Banker: A Story of Failed States, Financial Crisis, and the Wealth and Poverty of Nations.* New York: Penguin Press.

Mamdani, Mahmood. 1976. *Politics and Class Formation in Uganda.* Kampala, Uganda: Fountain.

Markus, Hazel Rose, and Shinobu Kitayama. 1991. "Culture and the Self: Implications for Cognition, Emotion, and Motivation." *Psychological Review* 98: 224–53.

Marshall, Ruth. 2009. *Political Spiritualities: The Pentecostal Revolution in Nigeria*. Chicago: University of Chicago Press.

Martin, Phyllis. 2009. *Catholic Women of Congo-Brazzaville: Mothers and Sisters in Troubled Times*. Bloomington: Indiana University Press.

Mauss, Marcel. (1925) 1990. *The Gift: The Form and Reason for Exchange in Archaic Societies*. Translated by W. D. Halls. London: Routledge.

Maxwell, David. 1998. "'Delivered from the Spirit of Poverty?' Pentecostalism, Prosperity and Modernity in Zimbabwe." *Journal of Religion in Africa* 28: 350–73.

Mayblin, Maya. 2010. *Gender, Catholicism, and Morality in Brazil: Virtuous Husbands, Powerful Wives*. New York: Palgrave Macmillan.

———. 2012. "The Madness of Mothers: Agape Love and the Maternal Myth in Northeast Brazil." *American Anthropologist* 114 (2): 240–52.

Mbembe, Achille. 2001. *On the Postcolony*. Berkeley: University of California Press.

McBrien, Richard P. 1994. *Catholicism*. San Francisco: Harper Collins.

Merton, Thomas. 1955. *No Man Is an Island*. London: Hollis and Carter.

Meuwissen, Liesbeth Emm. 2002. "Problems of Cost Recovery Implementation in District Health Care: A Case Study from Niger." *Health Policy and Planning* 17 (3): 304–13.

Meyer, Birgit. 1999. *Translating the Devil: Religion and Modernity among the Ewe in Ghana*. Trenton, NJ: Africa World Press.

Miguel, Edward. 2009. *Africa's Turn?* Boston: MIT Press.

Miller, Joseph Calder. 1988. *Way of Death: Merchant Capitalism and the Angolan Slave Trade, 1730–1830*. Madison: University of Wisconsin Press.

Miller, Katherine. 2013. "Lighting the Masjid: The Moral Pleasures of Labor in the Hunza Valley." Paper presented at Reed College, February 20.

Ministry of Finance, Planning and Economic Development, Uganda Participatory Poverty Assessment Process, and Centre for Basic Research. 2007. *Moving Out of Poverty: Understanding Freedom, Democracy and Growth from the Bottom Up*. Kampala: Ministry of Finance, Planning and Economic Development and Centre for Basic Research.

Mitchell, Bruce. 1998. *Resource and Environmental Management*. Harlow, UK: Longman.

Miyazaki, Hirokazu. 2004. *The Method of Hope: Anthropology, Philosophy and Fijian Knowledge*. Stanford, CA: Stanford University Press.

———. 2008. "Economy of Dreams: Hope in Global Capitalism and Its Critiques." *Cultural Anthropology* 21 (2): 147–72.

Moore, Henrietta. 2011. *Still Life: Hopes, Desires, and Satisfactions*. Cambridge: Polity Press.

Moore, Sally Falk. 1994. *Anthropology and Africa: Changing Perspectives on a Changing Scene*. Charlottesville: University of Virginia Press.

Moorman, John R. H. 1968. *A History of the Franciscan Order from Its Origins to the Year 1517*. Oxford: Clarendon Press.

Morduch, Jonathan. 1999. "The Microfinance Promise." *Journal of Economic Literature* 37 (December): 1569–614.

Mosse, David. 2004. "Is Good Policy Unimplementable? Reflections on the Ethnography of Aid Policy and Practice." *Development and Change* 35 (4): 639–71.

Nguyen, Vinh-Kim. 2010. *The Republic of Therapy: Triage and Sovereignty in West Africa's Time of AIDS*. Durham, NC: Duke University Press.

O'Neill, Kevin Lewis. 2010. *City of God: Christian Citizenship in Postwar Guatemala*. Berkeley: University of California Press.

Ong, Aihwa, and Stephen Collier, eds. 2005. *Global Assemblages: Technology, Politics, and Ethics as Anthropological Problems*. Malden, MA: Blackwell.

O'Reilly, Kathleen. 2010. "The Promise of Patronage: Adapting and Adopting Neoliberal Development." *Antipode* 42 (1): 179–200.

Orley, John. 1970. *Culture and Mental Illness: A Study from Uganda*. Nairobi: East African Publishing House.

Orta, Andrew. 2004. *Catechizing Culture: Missionaries, Aymara, and the "New Evangelization."* New York: Columbia University Press.

Paley, Julia. 2001. "The Paradox of Participation: Civil Society and Democracy in Chile." *PoLAR: Political and Legal Anthropology Review* 24 (1): 1–12.

Parry, Jonathan. 1986. "The Gift, the Indian Gift and the 'Indian Gift.'" *Man* 21 (3): 453–73.

Piot, Charles. 2010. *Nostalgia for the Future: West Africa after the Cold War*. Chicago: University of Chicago Press.

Poovey, Mary. 1998. *A History of the Modern Fact: Problems of Knowledge in the Sciences of Wealth and Society*. Chicago: University of Chicago Press.

Power, Michael. 1997. *The Audit Society: Rituals of Verification*. Oxford: Oxford University Press.

Prest, A. R., and R. Turvey. 1965. "Cost Benefit Analysis: A Survey." *Economic Journal* 15 (300): 683–735.

Quade, Edward S. 1971. "History of Cost-Effectiveness." In *IFORS International Cost-Effectiveness Conference*. Washington, DC: Rand Corporation.

Rabinow, Paul. 2003. *Anthropos Today: Reflections on Modern Equipment*. Princeton, NJ: Princeton University Press.

Rahnema, Majid. 1992. "Participation." In *The Development Dictionary: A Guide to Knowledge as Power*, edited by W. Sachs, 116–31. London: Zed Books.

Redclift, Michael. 1987. *Sustainable Development: Exploring the Contradictions*. New York: Methuen.

Redfield, Peter. 2010. "The Verge of Crisis: Doctors Without Borders in Uganda." In *Contemporary States of Emergency: The Politics of Military and Humanitarian Interventions*, edited by Didier Fassin and Mariella Pandolfi, 173–95. Brooklyn, NY: Zone Books.

———. 2012. "Doctors, Borders, and Life in Crisis." *Cultural Anthropology* 20 (3): 328–61.

Rieff, David. 2002. *A Bed for the Night: Humanitarianism in Crisis*. New York: Simon and Schuster.

Riles, Annelise. 1998. "Infinity within the Brackets." *American Ethnologist* 25 (3): 378–98.

———. 2000. *The Network Inside Out*. Ann Arbor: University of Michigan Press.

Rist, Gilbert. 2003. *The History of Development: From Western Origins to Global Faith*. London: Zed Books.

Rivkin-Fish, Michele. 2011. "Learning the Moral Economy of Commodified Health Care: 'Community Education,' Failed Consumers, and the Shaping of Ethical Clinician-Citizens." *Culture, Medicine, and Psychiatry* 35 (2): 183–208.

Robbins, Joel. 2004. *Becoming Sinners: Christianity and Moral Torment in Papua New Guinea Society*. Berkeley: University of California Press.

———. 2007. "Continuity Thinking and the Problem of Christian Culture: Belief, Time, and the Anthropology of Christianity." *Current Anthropology* 48 (1): 5–38.

Rose, Nikolas. 1999. *Powers of Freedom: Reframing Political Thought*. Cambridge: Cambridge University Press.

Rostow, Walt Whitman. 1960. *The Stages of Economic Growth, a Non-Communist Manifesto*. Cambridge: Cambridge University Press.

Rousseau, Jean-Jacques. (1762) 1979. *Émile, or On Education*. Translated by Allan Bloom. New York: Basic Books.

Scherz, China. 2013. "'Let Us Make God Our Banker': Ethics, Temporality, and Agency in a Ugandan Charity Home." *American Ethnologist*. 40 (4): 624–36.

Sachs, Jeffrey. 2005. *The End of Poverty: How We Can Make It Happen in Our Lifetime*. New York: Penguin.

Schoenbrun, David Lee. 1998. *A Green Place, a Good Place: Agrarian Change, Gender, and Social Identity in the Great Lakes Region to the 15th Century*. Portsmouth, NH: Heinemann.

Schultz, Theodore W. 1960. "Value of U.S. Farm Surpluses to Underdeveloped Countries." (Proceedings of the Annual Meeting of the American Farm Economics Association.) *Journal of Farm Economics* 42 (5): 1019–30.

Scott, James C. 1998. *Seeing Like a State: How Certain Schemes to Improve the Human Condition Have Failed*. New Haven, CT: Yale University Press.

Sharma, Aradhana. 2006. "Crossbreeding Institutions, Breeding Struggle: Women's Empowerment, Neoliberal Governmentality, and State (Re)formation in India." *Cultural Anthropology: Journal of the Society for Cultural Anthropology* 21 (1): 60–95.

Shweder, Richard, and Edmund Bourne. 1982. "Does the Concept of the Person Vary Cross-Culturally?" In *Cultural Conceptions of Mental Health and Therapy*, edited by A. J. Marsella and G. M. White, 97–137. Dordrecht, Holland: Reidel.

Simpson, Anthony. 2003a. *"Half London" in Zambia: Contested Identities in a Catholic Mission School*. Edinburgh: Edinburgh University Press for the International African Institute.

———. 2003b. "Personhood and Self in Catholic Formation in Zambia." *Journal of Religion in Africa* 33 (4): 377–400.

Smith, Daniel Jordan. 2004. "Contradictions in Nigeria's Fertility Transition: The Burdens and Benefits of Having People. "*Population and Development* 30 (2): 221–38.

Smith, Philip B., and Eric Thurman. 2007. *A Billion Bootstraps: Microcredit, Barefoot Banking, and the Business Solution for Ending Poverty*. New York: McGraw-Hill.

Sniegocki, John. 2009. *Catholic Social Teaching and Economic Globalization: The Quest for Alternatives*. Milwaukee, WI: Marquette University Press.

Stewart, Pamela J., and Andrew Strathern. 2001. "The Great Exchange: Moka with God." *Journal of Ritual Studies* 15 (2): 91–104.

Stirrat, R. L., and Heiko Henkel. 1997. "The Development Gift: The Problem of Reciprocity in the NGO World." *Annals of the American Academy of Political and Social Studies* 554: 66–81.

Stoneburner, Rand L., and Daniel Low-Beer. 2004. "Population-Level HIV Declines and Behavioral Risk Avoidance in Uganda." *Science* 304 (5671): 714–18.

Strathern, Marilyn. 2000. *Audit Cultures: Anthropological Studies in Accountability, Ethics, and the Academy*. New York: Routledge.

Swidler, Ann, and Susan C. Watkins. 2007. "Ties of Dependence: AIDS and Transactional Sex in Rural Malawi." *Studies in Family Planning* 38 (3): 147–62.

———. 2009. "Teach a Man to Fish": The Sustainability Doctrine and Its Social Consequences." *World Development* 37 (7): 1182–96.

Taubes, Jacob, and Aleida Assmann. 2004. *The Political Theology of Paul*. Stanford, CT: Stanford University Press.

Tiberondwa, Ado K. 1998. *Missionary Teachers as Agents of Colonialism: A Study of Their Activities in Uganda, 1877–1925*. Kampala: Fountain.

Ticktin, Miriam Iris. 2011. *Casualties of Care: Immigration and the Politics of Humanitarianism in France*. Berkeley: University of California Press.

Tsing, Anna. 2005. *Friction: An Ethnography of Global Connection*. Princeton, NJ: Princeton University Press.

Uganda Bureau of Statistics. 2002. Uganda Population and Housing Census.

Uganda National NGO Forum. 2009. "The NGO Sector in Uganda, Its Operating Environment and Relationship with Government: A Brief for a Meeting between Representatives from the NGO Sector and the 3rd Deputy Prime Minister and Minister of Internal Affairs—Hon. Kirunda Kivejinja."

Vansina, Jan. 1990. *Paths in the Rainforests: Toward a History of Political Tradition in Equatorial Africa*. Madison: University of Wisconsin Press.

Vokes, Richard. 2005. "The Kanungu Fire: Millenarianism and the Millennium in Southwestern Uganda." In *The Qualities of Time: Anthropological Approaches*, edited by David Mills and Wendy James, 301–14. Oxford: Berg.

Wallerstein, Immanuel. 1979. *The Modern World System*. New York: Academic Press.

Wanyama, Olandason. 2009. "Gov't Bans NGO Seminars in Karamoja." *New Vision*, April 19. http://www.newvision.co.ug/D/8/12/678602.

Wardlow, Holly. 2004. "Anger, Economy, and Female Agency: Problematizing 'Prostitution' and 'Sex Work' among the Huli of Papua New Guinea." *Signs* 29 (4): 1017–40.

———. 2006. *Wayward Women: Sexuality and Agency in a New Guinea Society*. Berkeley: University of California Press.

Weber, Max. 1904. "'Objectivity' in Social Science and Social Policy." In *The Methodology of the Social Sciences*, edited by Edward A. Shils and Henry A. Finch, 49–112. Glencoe, IL: Free Press.

———. 1978. *Economy and Society*. Berkeley: University of California Press.

———. 2002. *The Protestant Ethic and the Spirit of Capitalism*. New York: Penguin.

Weil, Simone. 1973. *Waiting for God*. New York: Harper and Row.

Weisgrau, Maxine K. 1997. *Interpreting Development: Local Histories, Local Strategies*. Lanham, MD: University Press of America.

Weiss, Tara. 2007. "Performance Philanthropy." *Forbes*, January 3, last accessed March 27, 2013, http://www.forbes.com/2007/01/03/leadership-charity-philanthropy-lead-citizen-cx_tw_0103geneva.html.

West, Paige. 2006. *Conservation Is Our Government Now: The Politics of Ecology in Papua New Guinea*. Durham, NC: Duke University Press.

Wiegele, Katharine L. 2005. *Investing in Miracles: El Shaddai and the Transformation of Popular Catholicism in the Philippines*. Honolulu: University of Hawai'i Press.

World Bank. 1998. *Beyond the Washington Consensus: Institutions Matter*. New York: Oxford University Press.

World Commission on Environment and Development. 1987. *Our Common Future*. Oxford: Oxford University Press.

Wrigley, Christopher. 1964. "The Changing Economic Structure of Buganda." In *The King's Men*, edited by Lloyd Fallers, 16–63. New York: Oxford University Press.

Zigon, Jarrett. 2008. *Morality: An Anthropological Perspective*. Oxford: Berg.

———. 2011. *"HIV Is God's Blessing": Rehabilitating Morality in Neoliberal Russia*. Berkeley: University of California Press.

CPSIA information can be obtained
at www.ICGtesting.com
Printed in the USA
LVHW02s1056190118
562903LV00004B/15/P